WHY I THINK DIFFER

FINDING A CALLING

CHELLAGANAPATHY

DEDICATION

I dedicate my book to,

Those who want to change their life in the trap of middle class and slavery life thoughts.

Contents

Preface

According to India's national council for applied economic research, the people who earn 2,00,000 – 10,00,000 per annum are considered the middle class. Mostly 90% of Indian population are middle class, they earn an average of less than 25000 monthly. There are more than 45 cores of people in India who are searching for jobs.

According to happyness.me 2022 report,it surveyed 1360 Indian employees from all over India ,nearly 59% of employees don't like there jobs and are not happy at their work. Part-time employees are also less happy than those who are employed at full-time.

Where people can't like their job,why do they want to go it? Because of their expenses or poor programming

Why some people can succeed in their life and others not? Studying hard and getting a high-paying job to create value in their life?

Ok! Getting a job is a good idea for money earning, did you notice about income tax rates?

Investing in index funds makes you rich, at which age, at 60 or 80?

Nearly,72% of students in college tell they have poor customer service, which means college can't provide value to their time,

Why does this happen? Is our educational system failing? Or are OUR THINKING PATTERNS failing?

The survey conducted by Deloitte shows, that of 3000 full-time workers in the US only 20% are passionate about their work, think about 80% OH! It was a trap, many of them can't like their job, they just go for

MONEY!

BRAINSTORMING TRUTH

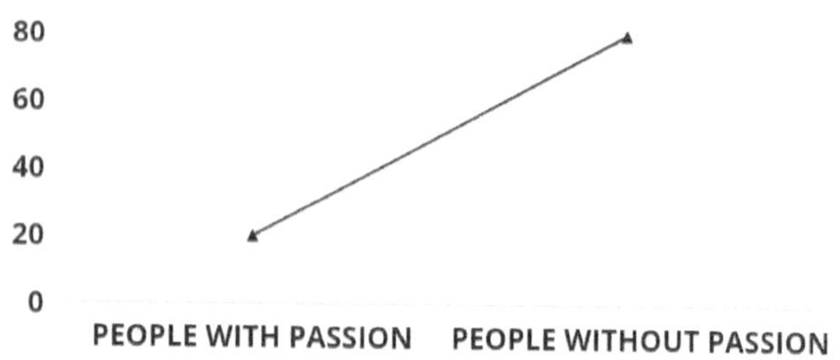

PASSION TRUTH

Think about, how these less passionate people contribute to our economy to the next level[NO WAY]

Why does this happen? Why people can't follow their passion?

Let me ask a personal question if you are a married employee answer it

What type of marriage is your's[love or arrange marriage], where your answer is a love marriage, I ask you a simple question,

HOW MANY HOURS HAVE YOU SPENT ON YOUR LOVED ONES?

HOW MANY DAYS DID YOU GO ON THE VACATION WITH YOUR LOVED ONES?

When I try to answer this question,

You only have 24 hours a day, as an employee, you sleep 8 hours a day, so one-third of your time vanishes in your sleep, then you have only 16 hours in your hand,

Yeah! You have some personal activities[that take 5 hours a day]so, you have only 11 hours on your hands.

If you are 9-5 jober, you have 8 hours of work in your office, so 11-8= 2 hours, only 2 hours in our hands[eliminate these 2 hours for travel, and other job activities]

At final you have 0 hours to spend time with your loved ones. Then why do you spend a ton of hours developing a relationship that you like?

This was the major concern in middle-class life

Just imagine FAMILY STRESS + JOB STRESS = DEPRESSION, which makes HUMAN LIFE INTO DEVIL LIFE.

They have no hours to spend on their loved ones[except sunday], and they sacrifice 6-day work and 1 day of enjoying, many of them tell Sunday is a wonderful day in my life.

I ask why. Because they said it was a holiday, then I asked you to spend these 6 days as a holiday, they don't have an answer to reply!!!

They are programmed to be poor, and simply follow the rules where that society creates for them.

They can't change their lives because when they change, their circle of influence tells them, they are taking a risk![risk was the dangerous word in the middle-class dictionary]

So, they live their life in a stagnant manner, they can't change that influences their generation also.

Another one- is when I ask college students, why did you choose this course? what purpose that you choose this course?

Their replies are priceless because they can't know, why they choose this course. After all, they can't know their calling.

They simply follow their parent's words, like going to school, and getting good grades that make them get high-paying jobs that create lifetime settlements.

Let me ask one question, Does a job makes you rich?

Just go to the Forbes magazine website, see the top billionaire list, where any employee or a job seeker on this list

NO! The list of billionaire names are not an employee, they are entrepreneurs, and they have value in their life, they can't follow what their mom and pop saying to them, they create their own life by their CALLING!!

JOB CAN'T MAKE YOU RICH BUT YOUR PURPOSE LEADS!

you can see the inequality graph also,

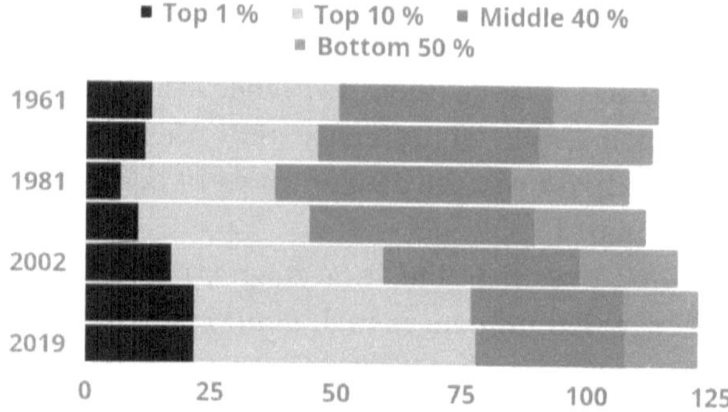

INEQUALITY IN INDIA

How top 10% make a more than 50% of income than a middle class

is there any secret formula or there think patterns?

If you are a guy who wants to know, how the middle class can change their life into becoming rich [financially free]

This book will show you.

It can change your thinking patterns, via the accurate data I provide in this book, by analyzing the data

You get value for your life

Noted it – we have all rights to enjoy our life, to live an extraordinary personal life, or live a luxurious life, have good sex, or any else

It came to reality, don't listen to other people, those who are told to limit your belief because we are MIDDLE CLASS

Life can change, once you believe

My life changed, when I believed, Everything starts with our mindset, once you develop a strong mindset, it will pay off

Caution – I can't write this book for motivation, I only write for people who want to escape the middle class and create value in their life.

Noting is impossible, again

WE LIVE ONLY ONCE ON THE EARTH, SO NEVER SACRIFICE OUR PRECIOUS LIVES TO ANYONE!

Those who want to change the middle-class life, take a pen in your hand and underline every line you aspire because a tiny new thing can grab an ocean in the long term, note it

Let's move on......

Middle Class Mania

When a person whose born into the middle class, always think about the external world with a ton of money in his hands, He speaks about various successful peoples and their struggles

what is the main concern is THINK ABOUT RICH AT ALL DAY, can change their life, it depends on how they dreamed, are they dreamed in their heart truth with a true work ethic, they go to the ladder of success.

But ...... GUESS WHAT

Only 5 to 10% of the middle-class population can achieve this victory, but what happens to 90% of peoples

When you speak to them, their core values are

► LIVE A STAGNANT LIFE

► PRAY A GOD FOR AN HOUR

► WATCHING ENTERTAINMENT AND TV SHOWS AT A NUMBER OF HOURS

► SPREADING GOSSIP ABOUT THEIR COMMUNITY

► WORK FOR MONEY

These are the main slogan they tag on their mind.

When raising their kids,

You may be surprised because of their core belief

► STUDY HARD

► GET GOOD MARKS

► ADDITIONAL TIME FOR TUITION

► HIGH-PAYING JOB

► LIFE TIME SETTLEMENT

This was the core belief they pass down from generation to generation....

When you break this belief, you are considered as a CROOK on their community, it was total *******....

COLLEGE AS A CRIME

Parents define 'COLLEGE' as a four-year bachelor's degree program, that helps their children to get a high-paying job

Many students, even didn't know, why they join this course or this college, they tell, my mom tells or my father tells or my relatives tell to join this course.

Then I ask, why your mom or father or relatives recommend this course, They tell, because of HIGH PAYING JOB!!!!!!!!!!!!!!!!!!

Then I ask, why do you need a high-paying job, They reply, when I earn a high salary that leads my life into a luxury fit, where I can build my dream house, Buy my favorite car and marry a gorgeous girl.

But most of the students even didn't know about the taxation of India that create a disaster output at last, when they earn a high salary.

[I explain taxation in the latter chapters, which helps a middle-class boy to aim high]

Most the peoples join college, without purpose, they just enjoy their time with their friends without worrying about future

When I ask them, they reply, ENJOY THE PRESENT BRO !!!!

Thinking about when you skip 5 seconds in your life before you skip, you are in present, but after your skip, the 5 seconds are passed, and we can't go it.

Just imagine, you are living a hard middle-class life, but masking the poverty at the love of your friendship in your college but the four-year program or 3-year program, or a diploma at[2-year program], Everything change in a 5 seconds

When your future is in your present, Nothing will happen, and the same poverty tags on your mind But once your college is finished, your friends break down into separate parts, the final emotion last, when they leave and two to three-day loneliness are fall but Guess what!

Nothing change, you live the same life where you have in before entrance to the college program

You feel about poverty and gossip about your illness to another illness guy, to relieve their pain!!!

This was the story of every middle-class boy's face!!!!

You can enjoy the present but the future is not a big bypass, it was in a matter of seconds travel, so, always prepare for this!!!!

NO CALLING NO GROWTH

Many students enter college for degree certifications, they even didn't know their calling in their college

Imagine, a pilot who doesn't like to drive a plane, he only drives because of high paying paycheck, In simple terms, He can't like to be a pilot, he just drives because of his salary

Can you trust this person, to give your precious life, NO WAY

There is a huge difference between people with passion and people without passion

That gives different output than you ever imagine.

WHY PEOPLE CAN'T FIND THEIR CALLING OR THEIR PASSION?

The answer is so simple, because of manipulation

Most people are manipulating their minds with the persuasive words of their parents and relatives, Their words make them close their thinking power and open their follow-up mind, and just follow the words are they telling.

People in this condition was unconscious, they can't know what will happen in their life, and they just follow the rules, that their parents and relatives sketch for them.

Blocking their thinking power that reduces their spirit voice or inner voice cancels their calling and makes them like a brain without power.

Passion or calling always comes through their inner voice, when people cancel their calling or their inner voice, I bet they lose their entire life and live a life for someone else

A PROGRAMMING MANTRA

Most middle-class families have programmed their mantra to the child at their initial stages, This makes them lose their mind

Imagine, when a teacher teaches a lesson,[if anyone reading this book, can have the courage to approach a teacher, to ask a doubt about the external syllabus of your topics]

Anyone!

If you ask, I bet, you are the innovator

But my focus is on The people who didn't ask a doubt, Why it will happen,

Some following points

►when we ask doubt, teachers bite us

► When we ask a doubt, our friends tease us

► prestige problems

► Girlfriend's eyes

Yeah! These are things you think when you ask a doubt, these points close your mind and just follow up on what the entire students do!

That leads to the biggest error in your future, By following another mantra that always leads our life into the biggest trap

It makes your inner voice silent and on long days, Your INNER VOICE IS ABSENT,

Then, EVERYTHING IS finished!!!

You live in a trap, NO!!

You live in a RAT RACE at life long zone.

It leads your calling to the existing zone.

CAN I CHANGE THESE PATTERNS

Yes! Definitely

This is why! I write this book

This book helps you to change your thinking, Why think instead of a dream life?

Because everything occurs first on our thinking patterns, Once you have a good thinking pattern that leads your life into pleasant

I explain various tactics that help to see a middle-class man thinking into a rich one

I can't tell you to get to meditate and get results, I proved this method with mathematical formulas that help you see the good insights instead of meditating in a prolonged manner for richness

I bet you! Once you read this book, you can see a different thinking pattern in your approach!!

Always remember,

'YOUR THINKING INFLUENCES YOUR ACTION,

YOUR ACTION INFLUENCES YOUR DESTINY'

- Nitin Namdeo

Let's take a step to read this book, to change your destiny!

And again

'OUR TIME-LIMITED

JOYNESS AND HAPPINESS ARE THE ONLY THINGS THAT ACT AS A FUEL FOR OUR LIFE TRAVEL

NEVER SACRIFICE THESE TWO FACTORS FOR ANYBODY

MONEY IS NOT A PROBLEM

BUT OUR THINKING......'

Who Am I

I am chellaganapathy, a visionary man, here in this book, I share my life experiences with the world

so, why need to learn my life experiences

START WITH WHY is the wonderful skill that you want to evolve in this world.

The purpose of my life WHY is TO KNOWN MY CALLING

WHAT DO YOU MEAN BY CALLING?

The calling is the purpose that is created by your mind through your life visuals, or in simple words – the DAEMON of your spirit that speaks to you, to give a reason for your birth

In the teenage years of my life, I did not find my calling, I constantly searched here and there, for when my spirit started to speak to me

But it does not speak to me

Each day and night, I feel frustrated, by my calling

I always ask myself, What is the purpose of my life?

Why I am living?

Through constant questing myself, I have known MY CALLING and I evolve to get the confidence to get my dream

My prime motto for writing this book is to give the secret hacks that I followed in my rituals that help to see this world through a different lens whenever I see a lot of people, in my life who cut off their dreams and live in a fallacy world, to give every credit to god for the destiny

It was totally F*** . I don't use this world but there were a lot of bullsh*t people are collapsed their life and their generation

it causes me to temper,

Do you know how evolution sucks?

Following the same data and advice from core people that followed from generation to generation, without rational thinking.....

If anyone thinks rational ways, the community of the[bullsh*t peoples tell – you are psychic]

That depresses and de-motive the people's real character and their calling

It was sad to me,

because I also face this fallacy and poor generation rules

Once I know my calling, I evolve[i often use this world – because I like this word] on mindset to see the different views of the world

Like I see both head and tails of the coin, where I'm on the edge!

OK! Let's move on to the main parts

But I am sure bet you after you read this book, you change your mindset and your thinking patterns....

HOW I VIEW THE WORLD

CHAPTER ONE

HISTORY OF MINE

In this part, I am a school student, I am an above average student in my 7th grade, I collaborate with my friends and enjoy the joy of childhood with lots of emotions....

you know one quote, when we are in the same location for too long that becomes your *COMFORT ZONE*

That reduces your productivity,

So, my dad plans to shift me to another school for my higher education

on the occasion, I see a lot of new faces that make me a little panic! then I easily mingled with these people and today they are my best friends. In 8th grade it was going like a laughing face, I am like a programmed man, I don't have any rational thinking to know, just be foul and round on the world.

Throughout the journey of my 10th grade, where in my school, they have 4 sections of 10th grade, where 'A' section for toppers, 'B' section for people who are good at marks, and 'C' and 'D' for average and below average students

My dad told me, my son, you need to get the topper seat, I just look at him, and tell OK! Dad when I selected to topper seat[which means SECTION A] make I enjoyed the movement and felt proud of mine

through the following days and days, it just move in a fast manner like tests and tests on various subjects

my luck to get this section, where I see, how the quality of education interprets, then I make friends with this section. We enjoyed every moment with feeling love and trust.

The condition changed, when I have the skill to write a story and song lyrics, I LOVE MY CREATIVITY, the particular skill, I write more than 25 stories, and I give them to my friends and asked them for feedback.

They give good feedback and some worst but it helps to mature on the skill, where today it will pay off for me......

Then write a story skill that converted into the direction of the story, where I take a mobile and tripod, to shoot the film!

I think today, it was just funny things, but on the occasion, it was serious to become a director of my film,

I LOST MY LOVABLE PLACE

Where these are things that happen in my life, when I finish 12th grade, I comes to mature to get an answer to the world's best question, which every parent has asked their kids

But my mam and dad tells, me to get study MBBS[doctorate study], I just manipulative with my father's persuasive words, and I just study for the entrance exams, Luckily I get a passing mark[294 out of 720], But I can't select to the doctor study

In passing following days, I searched about AYUSH college in Kerala and tamilnadu[WHY- because in our culture, if any kid fail to doctor study their parents prefer them Ayush department]

Where I am a big fan of the Siddha and ayurveda medicine system, and I love KERALA very much, throughout my life incidents.....

Finally, one calling come from Trivandrum, Siddha college, where we were barely able to pay the fees of this college, as a middle-class family, it was hard to bear it

My dad supported me, but he told me, just move on

BUT I LOVE KERALA[IT WAS JUST A MIX OF MY HEART AND TEARS]

I suddenly hug the call sheet and tears that are flow from my eyes

I cried a lot....................

I think everything was finished......, during the time COVID was dancing on the streets

All the problems cause me sudden frustration.....

I didn't recover from this pain........

PROGRAMMING WAY

When my mom and dad tell me good words, where the words like

everything that acts on our life that has a purpose!

But on the situation, I just feel sad.....

Then my dad, suggested me, about pharmacy

I even didn't know this name often,

But my mind that I develop or my father programmed me for lucrative jobs[every middle-class boy that have the same feeling as I have]

For example – when my father, tells me about any profession, I just google it, like

WHAT IS THE SALARY OF THIS PROFESSION

where I searched, WHAT IS THE SALARY OF PHARMACIST IN INDIA?

WHAT IS THE SALARY OF A PHARMACIST IN THE USA?

IN DUBAI? IN UK?

Whenever my dad told me about any profession, I just do it and again and again

I just mentally plan, where I enter into this job, I make cores and cores of income[i just dream it and live a fallacy way of life]

Then I registered my name on Dpharm[DIPLOMA IN PHARMACY], to get the ladder of the pharmacist profession to get a CORES

when I was selected to MADURAI MEDICAL COLLEGE, on the occasion when everything was good

I tell myself, we are the NO 1 in the college and just study hard, we get the core income job......

CHAPTER TWO

THE MOTIVATING FACTOR

Where are my school years, I just go for motivational videos to upgrade myself and I enjoyed the process

whenever I feel tired, I just go for motivational videos, to stimulate me, then I go for biographies of highly successful people in this world like ELON MUSK, STEVE JOBS, JACK MA, BILL GATES, WARREN BUFFET, etc

when I see these people's stories, where I am inspired by and way of my life in the world that changed

I learn many pain points from highly successful people, though I found some habits, was very successful people in the world mastered it.

TETRA SWORD

Where you know, THE WAY OF OUR LIFE THAT ARE DESIGNED BY YOUR HABITS

YOUR HABITS THAT LEAD YOUR DESTINY.....

When I see highly successful people live

they have habits like

▶ READING BOOKS

▶ **MEDIATION**
▶ **PROPER DIET**
▶ **GOOD RELATIONSHIP**

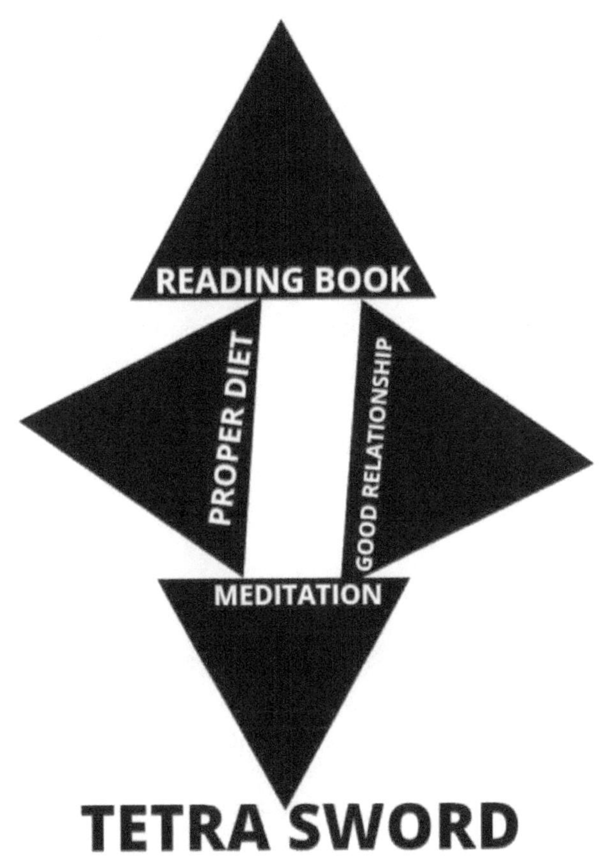

READING BOOK
PROPER DIET
GOOD RELATIONSHIP
MEDITATION
TETRA SWORD

I call it TETRA SWORD

MY UNDERSTANDING

through constant learning about successful people's lives, I go to the audiobook side, where I hear a lot of audio related to self-improvement

where at my age, I didn't memorize all things and was just barely able to remember them but I just hear, hear, hear!

And I noted many billionaires in the world are ENTREPRENEUR in nature, they have businesses at valued more than 500 billion dollars

and I see a lot about entrepreneurship and business people talks, that act as my MOTIVATING FACTOR

but I didn't know about the time, what is entrepreneurship?

I think, entrepreneurship is a job, where the handsome man with the navy blue suit, where he held a leather case in his hand that contains millions and millions of money!

I dreamed, what a life this is.........

MY YOUTUBE JOURNEY

by searching lot of details about every topic that enhances my curiosity to learn more and creates me to play a significant role in my role

In the following, where I create a youtube channel and create a blog, and I think once I post the video and write the blog I create a core!

I worked very hard, to search the content and post on youtube[i failed at my first two youtube channels and then one channel create me happiness[channel name – CG ZOO], where my video crosses 1k+ views[yeah it's not big, but as a kid, it was big enough for me]

every time, I record the video, many background voices are coming in and I irritate by these noises while recording.

Most noises come from my parents.................

Then, on some destiny move of my family, I quit YouTubing and everything is finished

YEAH! I AGAIN LOST MY LOVABLE THINGS

but I didn't blame my parents

Life is 100% responsibility for your actions.............

MY BLOG JOURNEY BEGINS

Where I create the blog[on blogger. com], where I create a 3 blogs

1 – for self developments

2 – for my stories

3 – for my pharma studies

I post more than 100 posts,

but what, NOTING WORKS.....................

The maximum number of views I get on my post is 100.

where on the occasion, I apply for GOOGLE ADS,

where it was also rejected, more than 15 times...

YEAH! I AGAIN FAIL AND LOOK FOR SOME NEW THING

Every time I fail, I learn some lessons that help me to see a different point of view my dad told me, why do you waste time on this type of stuff that causes nothing?

I didn't tell one word to my father.

I just prefer silence

I think it was the only one that acts my motivating factor.

TRUTH OF MOTIVATING FACTOR

Some motivational videos play an important role in my life

The titles of the videos are

SIDE EFFECTS OF MOTIVATION?

DO YOU NEED MOTIVATION FOR YOUR DREAM?

MOTIVATION DRUGS?

While watching these videos, I learn some new things and it's changed my view of this world

Motivation is just a force, that releases dopamine in your neurons to evaluate to reward us...

MOTIVATION SUCKS!

I see a lot of people have a motivating character, but when it comes to action, they fail

they tell, it was so hard or I worked 1 hour, so I need to take rest, where they go for motivation factor, they spent their time on the evil for 30 minutes or 1 hour and they work

They create this behavior in their habit rituals and they think it will pay off in the future,

But what is reality is they consume motivation as a 2hr entertainment movie

it causes them to feel sad and they tell, me that I work on my routine through motivation but it sucks!

The reason for this failure is, they depend on MOTIVATING FACTOR instead of their actions

MOTIVATION VS ACTION

2hr motivation and 30 minutes of actions can't provide efficient results.

you can get 1000 hr+ motivation but without a single step upward on your action, it reduces your rate of achievement, then the time spent on motivation is just an entertainment

Once I know this deep knowledge, where I avoid many motivational videos and I start to take actions

I failed a lot but through my search for new things that promote me something new

I soon learn more about action-taking tasks and I love it, where my motivating factor sucks, where the ACTION FACTOR IS raised....

WORDS MAY INSPIRE BUT ONLY
ACTION CREATES CHANGE
- SIMON SINEK

CHAPTER THREE

FACING REALITY

.

I START TO READ A BOOKS

When I quit my blog and youtube channels, I go across to searching for new things

Audiobooks helped me to see a different view of myself[I JUST PROGRAMMED MYSELF, I AM ALSO A SUCCESSFUL PERSON]

I BELIEVE IT ......

Then on hearing every book on self-development, they tell

Successful people are who productively spent their time and they get dead experiences from books

and they again tell, READING THE BOOK IS MORE SWEETER THAN HEARING BOOK,

then my mind strike, and tell to my body, IT WAS TRUTH!

Then I plan to read the book, I just searching, for which book is best for self-help growth

many of them suggest

7 HABITS OF HIGHLY SUCCESSFUL PEOPLE BY STEPHEN COVEY.

On initially I start reading this book, my mind tell to me, OH IT WAS DIFFICULT, PLEASE QUIT, GO MAN AND WATCH ENTERTAINMENT MOVIES

Yeah! I start to procrastinate reading this book,

REASONS ARE

I can't understand English

I can't focus my mind

while reading books, my mind floated on dreams, like luxury life, dream house, dream girl, etc

I think I procrastinate for nearly 3 months when the spider starts constructing his net house on my book!

Then a lot of motivation and motivating factors, when I get to start to read this book

My spirit guides me...

TALKING TO MY INNER VOICE[SPIRIT]

From my early teenage years to today, I have had a habit to speak to my spirit, I LOVE IT.

My spirits tell me, just read one page and tell the meaning to me

I tell, ok! Just one page, I think I will finish it in a few minutes

And my spirit asks me, what lesson did you learn from this...

I tell, self-development

my spirit tell, ok! cool[INITIAL IS HEAVY, ONCE YOU START EVERYTHING IS SMOOTH]

while I read the first page, I didn't get any words, because I can't understand it effectively.

Then I tell my spirit, YEAH! MAN, I CAN'T UNDERSTAND ENGLISH EFFECTIVELY,

he tells me, just improve your vocabulary knowledge, it will pay off

During my teenage years onwards, I have a curiosity to learn something new that works on same on vocabulary skills

I developed it and I worked hard, but finally, it pay off for me.

then I increase my page count

like 20 pages for 60 minutes

I start reading the books each by each line and remember it[I have a good memory to remember it]

KEY TAKEAWAYS I LEARN FROM THIS BOOK

[1] don't be a reactive guy, be proactive, to take 100% responsibility for your own life

[2] prioritize your time effectively, you must understand, which is important, urgent, and unimportant

[3] Think win-win situation[I commonly used this habit in my business]

[4] delegate your work and cooperation is pay off

cooperation is the only thing that helps humans to get evolved in the strange the world that helps to create innovation, today we just have...

These are the things that I learn from this book, but my life changed?

Mm mm!, yeah at a good amount but I get a little amount on this book[on my first reading but through forward I read this book 2-3 times, where It gives a different dynamic approach, today these habits are my keystones]

Ok! Through facing the reality of my life, I just get 1% growth in my life and have the happiness to finish my

first book
Then my spirit tells, OK! CG YOU ARE GETTING IT LET'S MOVE ON NEXT BOOK!
I tell, ok! MAN

THE COLLECTION OF BOOK JOURNEYS BEGINS

Then I searched self-help books on Flipkart, I usually prefer combo offer books
where I find a combo of four books at the rate of 399
the books are[many of them know this was a teasury]
[1] HOW TO WIN FRIENDS AND INFLUENCE PEOPLE BY DALE CARNEGIE
[2] THINK AND GROW RICH BY NAPOLEON HILL
[3] THE POWER OF OUR SUBCONSCIOUS MIND BY DR JOSEPH MURPHY
[4] THE RICHEST MAN OF BABYLON BY GEORGE CALSON
When I start reading this book[initially stages, I can't understand the terms, but my spirit tells me, NO EXCUSES, AGAIN READ AND GET A GEM.
So I focused heavily on books and then finally get a gem, each book change my life to something differ
I learn how to approach people, and how to think big from this book(1 and 2)
but the gem Is the power of our subconscious book,
In my school days, I have a big belief in god[religion-oriented things], but while reading this book, everything is changed
I then knew, my subconscious is everything, it controls my life and my decisions, and it creates a big impact on my life

when I have a fever or any disease, my mom prays the god and tells me, everything is normal

while reading this book and thinking about these thoughts, then I understand, my mom prays not on god but on her subconscious mind

when my mom projects his taught on her subconscious mind, with the strong belief, it will project on reality by the strong belief system of human

it was a LAW OF ATTRACTION[i explain later in this book]

where one section,dr murphy tells about mental healing, I think that dramatically changed my thinking about healing

this was the greatest treasure I get from this book, whenever I have a problem, I ask my subconscious mind to give the solution

it provides me.............

Today my life hugely improved by this subconscious thinking

I am easily healed by my mental things......

SKILL OF SHARE MARKET BEGINS

The last book in my 4 book collection is

THE RICHEST MAN OF BABYLON

when I read this book, I can't understand the words, because this book used hard English words[for me it was hard to understand]

then I plan to procrastinate

But my spirit scolded me, and tell, CG IF YOU CAN'T UNDERSTAND THE TERMS, GO AND GET THE HELP OF SOMEONE, IT WAS CALLED COOPERATION

I don't ask my mom and dad for this type of theory, so searched online, where I find the audiobook of this book

it was 1.30 hr audiobook, I hear it

Then my way of life that has changed heavily, and my financial IQ start to ride on my life

because I can't hear this topic often, I only focused on self-development but finance is a new topic to me, I learn more from this audiobook

KEY TAKEAWAY IS

[1] save 10% of your income

[2] invest your money

[3] get advice from people who are special in this field

[most people ask advice like

when people want to buy gold, many of them get advice from bricks maker instead gold makers]

through this understanding,

I search for investing topics

I taught investing means invest on our money in land or precious metals

But my curiosity teach me something different, where I get the gem of investing

it was so called SHARE MARKET

when initially days, people ask me, what is the share market?

A graph that contains green and red lines that are up and down due to the market oscillations

It was just a funny reply as a beginner of the share market, where I tell them!

Then my spirit tells me, If you want to become successful, you need to master this financial skill

so, I learn about the share market from youtube and I can't understand some terms like stock vs share, bonds vs debentures, what is Demat account, regulatory, etc then I search for people who are successful in the share market, where I found the legendary investor WARREN BUFFET, while seeing his life, I learn more new things

then one video, while I watching, he recommends INTELLIGENT INVESTOR BOOK, then buying it

but I can't understand a single term used in this book[because at the time, I am an amateur in finance]

But my spirit guides me,

I learn more from this book with the interlink of audiobooks, I get a core concept of investing

sorry ! VALUE INVESTING

[VALUE INVESTING means, buying a share with a value, not on market price]

I DEVELOPED STOCK-PICKING SKILLS

Investors buy the share at their intrinsic values or below the book value[if these terms are new to you, just search online, and you will get a gem]

soon I learn about three pillars of company performance

[1] income statement [also known as profit and loss account]

[2] cashflow statement

[3] balance sheet

then I learn more about these topics

through my financial IQ was improved,

My spirit tells me, to learn more about finance and the share market

then I find PETER LYNCH BOOKS

His view of finance influence me a lot, the thinking of a small boy to stock pick investor for example – if I buy a biscuit, I usually searched how many of them like this biscuit, and if the answer come under more than 1000, I prefer to invest in this company [BRITANNIA]

through I learn more about accounting via the share market and then economics, bank terminology, and management

then my life with the precious dream to become successful that begins......

The way of my maturity start to evolve

More finance knowledge improves my financial literacy and boosts my confidence in wealth building

before reading this book, when anyone asks me, how to be financially free, I just recommend going and getting a high-paying job

but today, if anyone asks me this question I reply........

[read on next chapter]

CHAPTER FOUR

BULLSH*T RULES

ROBERT KIYOSAKI VIEW

Where my book reading habit become a beast manner, I read lot and lot of books, where about the situation we are in the COVID CLIMATE, so everyone is isolated, it hugely helped me, to read a lot of books[HABIT -1 BE A PROACTIVE]

I find one book, namely CASHFLOW QUADRANT BY ROBERT KIYOSAKI

Before reading this book, my mindset was

study hard, get good grades in school, and get a high-paying job that pays me cores

This was the way, in which every middle-class people that were programmed

my father also plays this the same, he tells me, SON, YOU SHOULD STUDY HARD THEN YOU WILL GET A HIGH PAYING JOB

I just programmed these words, where my friends also...

MINDSET CHANGES

Then I read this book, it changed my mindset, view[whatever you call]

Robert Kiyosaki simply tells,

go to school, get a job, pay your taxes, save money and invest in the stock market that is programmed for poor

I was suddenly shocked by his view, because, I follow this principle from a kid to a teenage guy, and it broke my belief about society

then read this book, top to bottom

suddenly, suddenly,........

everything is changed, my NEW EYES WAS OPENED

then I realize, I followed BULLSH*T RULES from kid to my teenage, while this understanding, make me a different point of view

Robert Kiyosaki simply tells,

four quadrants, which are

[1] EMPLOYEE

[2] SELF EMPLOYEE

[3] BUSINESS OWNER

[4] INVESTOR

In this deep study of these quadrants,

I understand RICH PEOPLE DON'T WORK FOR MONEY, WHERE MONEY WORK FROM THEM'

it was paying me a lot,

and I get a clear definition of WEALTH, through Buckminister fuller,

DEFINITION OF WEALTH

wealth means when you stop working, how long you can survive in this world, this was the simple definition of wealth

then the following chapters, I understand

Rich people invest on time, whereas poor people invest in money

I can't breathe, while I reading these pages, because, it was opposite to my belief system

I ask my dad, as same as Robert Kiyosaki, my dad tells, go and get study, and don't waste your time

Then I see the answer of Robert Kiyosaki, in his books, I learn, that poor people hang on to expired information with their packet, if you can tell them, you are hanging on, they tell, YOU ARE CRAZY

this why the famous quote

'DON'T TEACH PIGS, BECAUSE IT ANNOYS YOU AND THE PIG'

I learn and see from Robert Kiyosaki's view what makes my destiny something differ

[note – I DON'T DISCUSS EVERYTHING I LEARN FROM THIS BOOK, BECAUSE IT WAS TON OF INFORMATION, IF YOU ARE LIKE THIS IDEAS, GO AND GET A BOOK THAT WILL PAY YOU ON LONG TERM]

SEE THE VERSES

My view of the world is to see the difference between rich and poor, healthy vs unhealthy

how rich people think vs how poor think

how rich people maintain relationships vs poor people maintain

how rich people get richer vs how poor people get poorer

Once, I see the differences, my way of perspective totally improved my eyesight from ordinary to extraordinary normally, people in the poor peer group often replicated the same principles, again and again, it was reproduced from generation, when you break the principle, everyone in the group tells, you are MAD!

So, most people can't break down their cultural belief and their principles, but the sad reality is most of them still follow these bullsh*t rules in today's modern world, they even didn't think rationally, about whether the belief that we follow generation, gives value or not!

I think most people in the modern world, have the same mindset in their kid to teenage years

it often comes from his family's behaviors

SAD REALITY

You know the famous quote from JIM ROHN

'YOU ARE THE AVERAGE OF FIVE PEOPLE YOU SPEND THE MOST TIME WITH

Yeah! It was the sad reality,

many peoples in the middle class, still follow their mom and dad's advice in their lives[it was just an example of THE RICHEST MAN OF BABYLON STORY – taking advice from a brick maker instead of a gold maker]

If you spent, your precious time with this type of average people, I will bet you, YOU ALSO A AVERAGE

Let's speak a simple example, I would want to ask you

[1] How do we take decisions in our life?

I wait for a few minutes when you people just answer it,

I will provide a box for this purpose.

BOX

ANSWER TO HARSH REALITY

HOW DO PEOPLE MAKE DECISIONS IN THEIR LIFE?

Based on our belief system, we make the decision based on the experiences that we gather from our life

you know people interpret movies with their life examples, it was the experiences they gather from the movie

For simple example – if you are in a conflict situation, you should want to make a decision, if not, you will come under tremendous pressure,

on the occasion, your brain interprets the ideas and experiences, we gather from our lifetime based on movies or people we meet or from reading books

where the same problem as you's, the movie star has, where the movie star plan well, executes it, and reduces his pressure, as per psychology, your brain tells you, we should do like that[means like movie star]

Why telling this is, because people use their experiences to make decisions in their life

if you have poor circumstances or poor people community, you often make decisions in a poor way

it was a harsh reality

you may ask how success comes to arise from the middle class.

I already tell successful people to invest their time in quality people, if the community doesn't contain this quality, they often go to the library for dead experiences.

WHAT ARE DEAD EXPERIENCES?

Dead experiences are gathered from books, where highly successful people leave their footprints in the papers of valuable books

Evolution is just one begins and other will die, as same as the rule of successful people lives, where dead is normal to anyone, so, most people have tons and tons of information, they prefer to write the experiences they face in their life on dairies

for example – Marcus Aurelius writes his daily experiences in his diary, that today helped as dead experiences[from the book MEDITATIONS]

Yeah! A man just imagines you get the cluster of experiences from the famous roman empire.

Once you understand they are perceptive, you will easily gain the dead experience, that helps you to make your decision effectively

Highly successful people often use these tactics, but none of the poor people know this[they often blame their community]

ANALYTICAL THINKING

Once you master this skill, you can easily make effective decisions in your life through analyzing the situation, you easily get the hidden sides of decision making

I often prefer HIGH-LEVEL THINKING[i will explain in later chapters]

Bullsh*t rules are often followed by these people, who don't have an analytical mindset, once you developed it, you easily break the matrix, where the poorest people are getting trapped.

I think you get a gem..........

Put in simple terms,

poor people who don't contain the skill of analytical thinking, simply follow other ordinary people for their life-effective decisions

rich people have the capacity, to analyze the situation and make the effective decision in their life, that will pay off them in the long terms

FINDING THE KEY

CHAPTER FIVE

FINDING MY CALLING

Through the evolution of books and dead experiences that make my perception of this world differ, I hugely influenced by Robert Kiyosaki and his workings

RICH DAD POOR DAD BOOK COMES ON

Then I ordered rich dad poor dad book in online, I have huge expectations from this book,

Guess what?

My way of life changes a lot, I think, I take a photo on his book page and post it on my WhatsApp status, where the lines in the photo are

'SCHOOLS ARE DESIGNED TO PRODUCE GOOD EMPLOYEES INSTEAD OF EMPLOYERS'

I soon understand the game changer, and I get the whole value of it....

HEY ! LET'S GO FLASHBACK

I didn't remember this day, but one night, when I had to sit down in my shop with the feeling of failure in the medical studies entrance exam

where my friend takes part in it, suddenly my father comes on, he also sits with us,

He asks me, son! What is your plan for your higher studies?

I have a dream about becoming an ENTREPRENEUR, through thinking of a navy suit with a leather suitcase[had millions and millions of money]

But I can't explain everything to my dad

while thinking about these dreams, my father recommended me to get study again and I'm not interested in medical studies[through the influence of many incidents, I can't prefer that]

my friend also recommends me, to get study medicals. Two forces [my father and friend[, had forced me to get into medical studies. I'm in a deep unconscious situation

what type of a decision, do I want to make?

I didn't know....

My father again asked this question

WHAT IS YOUR PLAN FOR YOUR HIGHER STUDIES

suddenly, my spirit answers the question with my unconscious nature,

I WANT TO BECOME AN ENTREPRENEUR!!!!!!!

My father laughed at me, and tell, IT WAS HARD, so go and get a good job that will give you security in your life

and he tells me, what is entrepreneurship?

I didn't have a good answer to tell him......

FIND MY CALLING

Through the evolution of book reading and seeing different perceptive of the world I easily see, I have something special

then I find my calling in my life

It was to become the great entrepreneur of southern Asia

But initially, I have a lot of fear to approach this big target, through my SPIRIT guided me, I GET THE MATURITY, that very few people in this world see it.

Then search for some spirituals, to control my fear and my mind oscillations, where I find PROKERALA.COM

where it provides some spiritual ideas, where I click on this website because of the name tag on KERALA, so I think it provides me a key.

When I see the LIFE PATH NUMBER SECTION, it for asks my date of birth, so just give it[07-07-2003], and it gives the result that shocked me!

THE RESULT

It gives

MY LIFE PATH NUMBER IS 1

the person with life path number 1 is a leader in nature, they have strong administrative skills and a lead team. People with these numbers are ENTREPRENEUR by nature, they have their businesses does have many employees working for them!!!!

Once I read this, there is some special force that penetrated my heart, my face glowing, I have a confident heartbeat, and my spirit tells, ALRIGHT ENTREPRENEUR, WELCOMES TO THE NEW WORLD.

I suddenly laughed and have a strength in my mind where I get my life value and purpose of the life...

[CONNECTION – but when I join the college[d pharm], I lost my spirit speech but after reading rich dad poor dad book, I taught, some force acting on my life, once I sense it, feeling the confidence to get approach my destiny problems..]

ENTREPRENEUR BY NATURE

As per Robert Kiyosaki's rules, an entrepreneur is a person who has a business, that gives free cashflow to him, which makes him financially free

they are on the business, not in their business, they create a system that gives him ton of money and time[yeah! TIME – VALUABLE ASSET]

I then start searching more about entrepreneurship, I learn more about business structure and their legal works

LET'S EXPLAIN SOME MAJOR DELIVERIES

WHY ENTREPRENEUR INSTEAD OF EMPLOYEE?

You know entrepreneurship, is a skill that you can develop from within, our school systems teach you to become an employee and self-employed, they train you to work for someone's dream, where they programmed you JOB SECURITY, HIGH PAYING JOB this type of lucrative words influence by many middle-class peoples

When you have a passion for employees, I think you waste the whole resource of your time to work for someone else life,

remember what is wealth definition, where you are in a job, your employer gives you a paycheck on every first day or his or her favorite day, where you are in the income tax slab, I think your paycheck breakdown into taxes, then you have in your hands

put into simple terms, where your work, you have a paycheck, isn't, everything is not!!

you invest your time in someone's dream and get a paycheck that deducts from taxes!!,you don't have the freedom to expose your ideas, you simply tap on the rat race, where every middle-class people trapped.

Many people tell me, CG, working at the top level, may give me a wonderful income

HAH! First, you should understand the INCOME TAX SLAB of India, then you decide, which is best...

For example – you are the top-level employee of XYZ COMPANY, where your salary is 8 cores,

just think, how much tax they put

according to today's IT SLOB, where you earn 8 core salary, where it taxes maximum at 3.39 cores[it was half of your income]

Let me explain this in detail,

You are a top-level employee of the XYZ company, and your monthly salary is approx 67 lakh, so the yearly amount is 8 cores[don't do the mathematical calculation, just imagine it]

Ok! Come to the main part, as per income tax slab rates,

TAX SLAB RATE FOR INDIVIDUAL

TAX SLAB RATE FOR INDIVIDUAL	
INCOME LEVELS	TAX RATES
[1] total income not exceed Rs.2,50,000	NIL
[2] Total income exceeds Rs.2,50,000 > Rs.5,00,000	5%[total income exceeds Rs.2,50,000]
[3] Total income exceeds Rs.5,00,000 > Rs.10,00,000	Rs.12,500 plus 20%[total amount exceeds Rs.5,00,000]
[4] Total income exceeds Rs.10,00,000	Rs.1,12,500 plus 30%[total amount exceeds Rs.10,00,000]

This is not a end,

Another one is Surcharge and HEC[Health and Education cess]

INCOME	SURCHARGES
Rs .0 – Rs.50 lakh	NIL
Rs.50 – Rs.1 core	10%
Rs.1 core – Rs.2 core	15%
Rs. 2 core – Rs 5 core	25 %
Above Rs.5 core	37%

Health and education cess – 4%

Let's calculate our CEO salary taxes[Rs.8 core]

INCOME LEVEL	SLAB RATE	TAX
Rs.0 to Rs.2,50,000	NIL	NIL
Rs.2,50,000 –	2,50,000 x 5%	12,500
Rs.5,00,000		
Rs.5,00,000- Rs.10,00,000	5,00,000 x20%	1,00,000
>Rs.10,00,000	7,90,00,000 x30% [8,00,00,000 – 10,00,00 = 7,90,00,000]	2,37,00,000
Tax lability		2,38,12,500
Add:SURCHARGE	2,38,12,500 x 37%	88,10,625
		3,26,23,125
Add:HEC	3,26,23,125 x 4%	13,04,925
Total tax lability		3,39,28,050

Income tax rate in india

It's ok to commit to this! And spend your valuable time on someone's dream, where you work hard and give 40% of your income to the government....

It's ok for normal people, but when's comes to leading a wonderful & financially freedom life, I think ENTREPRENEURSHIP IS THE ONLY SOLUTION

Where in this position, you have control of your life, when you create a system for your business, you don't need to work on it! it, you save your time and use it for some high-level things

Most billionaires in the world come into the category, they have a business, time freedom, financial freedom, and dream life to lead.

In the next chapter, you will learn more about business terms and books that read that changed my business knowledge.

FINISH WITH MY FAVORITE BY STEVE JOBS

'Your time-limited, so don't waste it living someone else's life

don't be trapped by dogma – which is living with the results of other people's thinking. Don't let the noise of other's opinions drown out your inner voice. And most important, have the courage to follow your heart and intuition'

- STEVE JOBS

CHAPTER SIX

WORK ON PROGRESS

In this chapter, I will tell more about business terminology, where I had learn.....

AFTER RICH DAD POOR DAD

After finishing rich dad poor dad, I searched for some books that related to business, where the advantage of reading books that gives reference section or author recommendation section, there I see the book name E-MYTH BY MICHEAL GABRIEL.

E-myth means entrepreneur myth, this book totally talks about business system building

KEY TAKEAWAYS

Micheal separates the business system into three parts

[1] technician

[2] manager

[3] entrepreneur

where each individual has separate roles,

for example – a technician, his work totally depend on technical

let's put in KISS[KEEP IT SUPER SIMPLE]

Where entrepreneur[CEO] has the vision to upgrade his business to the next level, and he approaches his manager for planning, then the manager of the business makes an effective plan, then they pass down to the technician, who works on the process to make the dream the happen.

This was the process he describes,...

Most people simply make mistakes in their business, whereas the entrepreneur of the business activities like a technician, put the plan and works on it, so what,there was no visionary, then the business sucks!

A lot of businesses failed for this one reason, without a system, your business fails, where you have a billion-dollar product but without an effective system, you are FAIL

With knowledge, I let see the difference between business and the system

Once you create an effective system, you need not work in your business, you just work on the business.

OWNING A BUSINESS OR JOB

Most people set up a shop, and they called as a business owner

IT WAS SILLY!

First, most people can't understand the difference between business and a job

Let me explain,

BUSINESS	JOB
Business have system	It doesn't contain system
You should on the business	You should in the business
You have time freedom	nil
System do all work	You do all work

Stress free method	Put your head heavy stress
When you stop working,your system gives money to you	When you stop working,you have no money
Tax on corporate rate	Tax at individual rate

BUSINESS VS JOB

Once you understand these differences, you will get a different viewpoint,

Most people are stuck in the shop, they act like technicians, managers, and entrepreneurs, once they stop working, they have no money flow, this is why it was called a job

Effective business means having a system that has a technician, manager, and entrepreneur, where each individual has some special duties, when these three forces are used effectively, YEAH! Your business has a reward...

This book's ideas make me feel something special, then with these key ideas, I learn more about business structures.

INNOVATION

In my teenage years, this word speaks to my heart, where the new creation totally depends on evolution.

Human life plays a major dominant role on the planet due to innovating new things that lead to making a big impact on the evolution of human civilizations

Lots of highly successful people have innovative production that makes them popular

For example – let's take ELON MUSK

he create some revolutionary companies that most people never imagined

like tesla, SpaceX, solar city, boring company,neuralink, open AI, etc

where each company has some specific innovation that puts new evolution, tesla changes entire motor units, SpaceX changes space myths, and open AI changes people's perception of artificial intelligence..

and so on...........

This type of learning leads me to create a special equation

INNOVATION → EVOLUTION

Then I read the book called ZERO TO ONE BY PETER THIEL

Where I learn, as same things again

when the company has a 1 to n approach, which means the company that participates in market share, where the company has a 0 to 1 approach, creates its own market[so-called MONOPOLY].

MONOPOLY

This type of business model is the king of the jungle, because, it controls everything in the market[especially – price], when people make demand their product, they are the only ones put their hands in the treasury box

Monopoly was created through INNOVATION, once you create an innovative product, that no one ever sees this or uses this, you create a MONOPOLY approach

It helps to gain a sustainable market share with high demand, it enhances your business into exponential route...

Through creating the monopoly, must understand that no one replicates your models, because there are a lot of crooks available in the marketplace

If you act in a polite manner, which means having a free approach due to creating an innovative production, within a matter of seconds, everything is collapse, because the competitor easily understands your tactics, then they implement their own innovative campaigns to penetrate their name in the market place where you created

So, as the monopoly, you should have a wide vision to attack the enemies, better to go with legal documents[like copyright, patent,trade mark, etc].

SIMPLE RULE FOR INNOVATION

Many people think innovation means doing 1000+ R&D works with hundred and thousand of dollars of investment, with highly talented people with their backups.

It was the answer, NO!

The simple rule for innovation is creating something new that no one ever sees in the market but they see in their daily activities

A little bit tricky right?

Yeah! Let me explain the simple manner

For example – where you have a coconut juice shop, your maximum selling price[let's take 100ml – INR 70 or 1 USD], where you have a lot of competition in your market

in this type of situation, you have a dream to earn good profit from this business against your competitors, what type of tactics you can use

Maybe you can increase your sales price or sales volume or equally summarize sales price and sales volume, on this strategy, you should understand your break-even point, most businesses fail to get their break even, so they get out of the businesses

Then what type of tactics you should to create the sustainable market share

simple – CREATE NEW PRODUCT[SO CALLED INNOVATING]

Just mix lemon with coconut water, or mint with coconut water, and you have a different product from your competitors

through education based selling[marketing strategy]

you explain the benefits of lemon with coconut water benefits

Like this copywriting message

Looking for refreshment

bored with coconut flavor

Thinking of new tastes

with tons of antioxidants

here that

lemon coconut juice is waiting for you!

It boosts your immunity

and assists digestion
that helps to fight with
world's most dangerous enemy
THANOUS!!!!!!!
OMG!

Once you create this type of innovative product with perfect marketing, I will bet you, that you create the destiny

'Innovation is simply creating the new one from an exciting one', where once you understand this, everything that stands for you......

NEXT MOVE

By getting a full understanding of innovation, I read the book[so-called – BLUE OCEAN STRATEGY]

Where in this book, the same innovation topic that explains like blue ocean strategy.

put into a simple summary

The author separates two oceans

[1] blue ocean

[2] red ocean

Blue ocean means they have an innovative product and they enter into the monopoly status that creates a new market share, where no one ever enters

But the red ocean strategy is just to fight with the market with an old product, using sales price drop or discount strategies, it will pay for short terms, but when it comes to long terms, everything fails.

Put simple words these meanings

where you have a dream to create a market for yourself, one thing that helps to get it[so-called innovation], where it leads to creating a sustainable market share for you[called monopoly], once you make it, you take the entire market with your uniqueness.

STAGNANT VS MOVEMENT

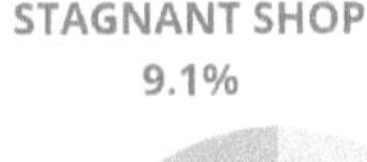

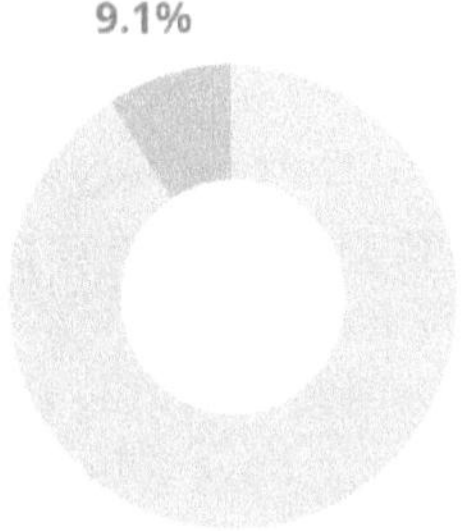

FRANCHISE VS STAGNANT SHOP

Most young entrepreneurs create innovative products but they have a more scale in their market palace

Let me explain this in detail

most physical business act in a stagnant manner, which means for example – you have a store or hotel, located in a town[the town have 1000 people]

let me ask you the question

where the total scale value of your market is 1000, where you have a dish or product at rupees 100, on total 1000[let's take 50% - 500 people buy it] where the total profit is 500*100 =50,000 only

this was the effect of stagnant stores

Let's look at movement,

movements mean DISTRIBUTION

SO-CALLED FRANCHISE MODEL

In simple terms, having a branch of your brand in different locations creates credibility with your customers which enhances your brand value.

when you have a quick service restaurant, this model of the franchise is best for you to get to scale your business

For example – for the same 100 rupee dish you have branches at different locations, where you have an opportunity to get scale your product with a large crowd

where you have 5 branches, and each branch has 500 customers, which means 100*500[dish*customer] = 50000, where you have 5 branches, then the net amount of your five branches is 50000*5 = 250000, YEAH! Just see how much difference where the business has on the MOVEMENT APPROACH.

Where you have a big manufacturing unit, It was so simple to scale your product through distribution channels[distributor – wholesaler -retailer]

THE MOVEMENT APPROACH is so simple for people who do have a business online, it was easy to scale with world internet users, and many eCommerce online platforms, use this tactic to scale their business at more than 100x

Once you developed your business at MOVEMENT APPROACH, it will bet you, you create your own destiny!!

CHAPTER SEVEN

MY COLLEGE DAYS

When I enter my college with huge pride, having a spirit of fire in my eyes, where my spirit tells me, YOU HAVE The POWER TO OUTSMART EVERYONE IN THIS COLLEGE but you just have to develop respect for your elders, where I get my spirit speech and move on the next part of life

SEARCHING FOR CORE MINDSET

During this stage of my life, my maturity is often below average, I can't understand, which type of people I am searching for!

I use COLD CALLING TECHNIQUES, where I can sell my belief to the rest of the college students

Guess what?

Nothing works,

where I get to see the people's eye view in their own perceptive, I just understand what type of core value everyone has!

Their core value is

GET GOOD MARKS

THAT LEADS TO GOOD CHARACTER

THAT GIVES A GOOD IMAGE

WHERE THE FINAL OUTPUT IS A CERTIFICATE
When I ask, a lot of people, why they join this college, they simply respond,
I searched a lot of professions, and finally, I get this, through my marks![PROUD MOVEMENT]
I laughed at these movements, where most people I met in this college have a poor core belief
They didn't have a life meaning
When speaking to these, I understand their values and their priorities
That helps me to see some special view
called WIDE VIEW

THE WIDE VIEW

You know I already told you about experiences
People I met in college, who have a poor experience In their life, most of them raised in a poor community, which means people with the poor core belief
They aim to live a normal life with little pleasure,
Once I see their perceptive, it was not their fault, it was also not their parent's fault, where the main fault comes from where they live.
where one has a good core belief but penetrates the bad community that collapses his entire productivity, where people evolve this type of community, the same bad belief follows people to people, which means generation to generation.
when I have this judgment in my head
I just ask them simple questions to justify by thinking
[1] do you have a dream to earn 100 core rupees?

Their answers make me justify my prediction at 100% where the answer

NO ! IT WAS BIG FOR ME, I JUST WANT GOOD PAYING GOVERNMENT JOB FOR THE REST OF MY LIFE

This thinking leads my wide eyes to open and make my maturity some thing peaks

On-time my spirit tells one thinking

CG! THE WAY OF EVERYONE LIFE

THAT DETERMINE BY THEIR ACTIONS!

TRY TO BREAK THE MATRIX

Where my college fellows they trapped in the matrix, where they tell me my life is awesome

Once I understand, I try to help them to see my own perceptive but it's not work

People have fear of my approach because they trapped in the matrix for more than 18+ years, when I speak them minutes words, it does not help them to see the difference

I then explain my own core belief in a detailed manner to these people,

GUESS AGAIN WHAT

nothing works,

Then I understand that life lesson I learned from the dead experience

EACH HEAD HAS AN EMOTION

Once I have a thinking of high level, where I miss the perceptive that people have in this world

What I mean is, every individual has some core belief that is come across their behavior, we can't erase this behavior until the individual mindset is changed

Everyone has some core belief that is bind in their mind effectively, where we can tell, I have a 100 core project, but no one responded because of their core values...

This understanding makes my perceptive different, this type of people can't trust us until we show actions

Once I get the key, I didn't waste my precious time on this type of people,

To conclude this topic

POOR PEOPLE OFTEN REACT TO EVENTS INSTEAD PROCESS

SOLITUDE APPROACH

Where people have their own core beliefs, I can't splash my thinking too lot, so instead of wasting time and energy

I just prefer SOLITUDE

That was the final approach we do in this community

I didn't feel sad, because I know 100 out of 99 people have the same core belief they pass down from generation to generation, they hesitate to update themselves, whereas the rest of one can't bind with this community, so the 1 % prefer solitude

When I know this, it was easy for me to act in solitude approach, I am not worried about this stuff. To my spirit guides me, every move I have taken from my life.

BENEFITS OF SOLITUDE

When I am in solitude, I have a lot of time on my watch to invest effectively to get the desired effect, and having silence in my mind creates a feeling of peace in my heart and my values

When I feel to communicate or share my feeling with anyone, I always prefer my books for this act, they listen to me with my spiritual care and they tell a lot of advice about my moves and the decision that the plan to implement

This type of maturity makes me feel, I AM SPECIAL, where I search for a lot of successful lives, where many of them follow the same tactics I follow in my life,

SORRY! I just follow their tactics,

Once I read STEVE JOBS BIOGRAPHY, I just see, where he outsmarted everyone in his community and he just fell into his teenage age, where I AM SPECIAL

This type of thinking and the way of evolution in my life leads me to something special.

TO INSPIRE OTHERS TO MAKE THEIR DREAM HAPPEN

Thorough my college days, I found a few rare people with have my core belief values, I just introduced myself and make a bond with this type of guy, where it helps me in the evolution of my life

My prime motto, which I just followed in my college days is

TO INSPIRE OTHERS TO MAKE THEIR DREAM HAPPEN

When I get to speak to these guys, I know their mindset and their values, once I get a key, I just explain to them, what is necessary for life with my style of language

That helps people to see my own perceptive and my values, when you give your values to the people, where the ton returns that waiting for you to get received.

I CHANGED MY FELLOW LIFE

Where I have a friend with a high vision but he didn't know what to do in his precious life, I just explain to my friend about JOB VS BUSINESS, FINANCIAL FREEDOM VS STRESSFUL LIFE[refer to previous chapters to understand more]

Once I planted the healthy seed in his mind, he evolve to see the difference and today he knows what type of things is necessary for his life to evolve.

UNKNOWN MEN TO INVESTOR

I already told you, .my prime motto is TO INSPIRE OTHERS TO MAKE THEIR DREAM HAPPEN

Usually, I went to my college by public transport [BUS], and I wait at my bus stand, You know me a lot, where I can't waste my time waiting for the bus

I just open youtube and listen to my finance subscription channels, where I see about the share market, suddenly a man comes, previous I see him on the bus.

Once I waiting at the bus stand and heard the updates on the share market, and that guy ask me, BRO! WHAT YOU ARE DOING?

His curious face speak me a lot, so I just tell my core beliefs to him, he just shocked, and ask me a lot of questions, I just listen to him and tell the truth about the society

His shocks again raise the peak and confidently see my eyes, I just simile him, and tell the truth of COMPOUND INTEREST.

COMPOUND INTEREST

What is compounding, it was the process of multiples, in simple terms, when you invest your money, where at the percentage of interest it was compounded, where the baby of interest again gets compounded and the baby's baby gets compounded, the process went on on on, until you quit!

This trick is majorly used by many professional investors, once you understand THE POWER OF COMPOUNDING, I bet you, IN YOUR LIFE, YOU NEEDN'T WORRY ABOUT MONEY IN YOUR ENTIRE LIFETIME.

Once I told him, he was shocked, and can't be recovered, then I mathematically explain this magic through the SIP CALCULATOR

MAGIC OF SIP

Sip means systematic investment plan, which means, you invest your money on month wards or week wards on the share market through the fund manager by the broker

An excellent fund manager of asset management companies invests your money on the share market, to get better returns for your savings[investment] that easily cross the inflation rates

For example – go to google and type top mutual funds in India, where you see a lot of fund houses with a lot of investments plan

Let's take I invest my savings in AXIS BLUE CHIP FUND,

my investment amount is 10,000 rupees in 2012, whereas in 2021, according to this 10 years, the fund generate 12.48%

Just go deep level,

2012	10000[*12 months] = 120000 + 837 return
2013	27360
2017	83404
2020	90989
2021	117953

Sip investment

This was the power of compounding

where in 2012 I invest 10000 in this fund, then 1 year I make a return of 837 rupees but through the long term 2021

I invest 1,20,000 but the return is 1,17,953 rupees so the total is 2,37,953 rupees [interest + principle]

Let's imagine I continue my investment for the next 20 years with the same interest rate of 12.4%

2021	1,17,953
2026	3,44,335
2031	8,15,010
2036	17,38,361
2041	35,00,534

Sip investment

In 2041, where my total investment amount is 3,60,000 rupees but my return is 35,00,534 so the total value is 38,60,534 rupees

This was the power of compounding. when I invest 3 lakh rupees from 2012 to 2041, where my return is 35 lakh rupees[interest only] it was known as the smart money

When I recommend this method, most of them were shocked, but this was the reality

DOES THE SHARE MARKET GAMBLE?

When we create a lot of awareness about mutual funds and share market-related terms, most people ask me simple questions

DOES IT GAMBLE?

I will just answer, WHAT IS GAMBLE?

Most people don't know the answer, then I explain

Gambling means that you don't know what will happen next, you just decide with an instant gratification approach

But intelligence means something different, they analyze,

BUSINESS

ECONOMY CYCLE

FINANCIAL MANAGEMENT OF BUSINESS

when you have an answer to forecasting the future, you call it gambling.

Analyzing the situation and making a decision is the essential skill of rationality, it was not gambling.

TEACH SHARE MARKET SKILLS TO MY TEAM MEMBERS

When you get a value on your life or know something new that changes a lot of people's lives, where the mature man decides to share his knowledge with the external world

I just share my knowledge with my friends with simple examples that make my friend's days pay off

I see the happiness in their eyes that makes me feel something special

According to Emerson, when someone breathes easier in their life because of your present, you succeed in your life

This level of thinking makes to share a lot of knowledge with my friends and my dead experiences

Today, my friend and I enjoy a lot in our lives and way of life games.

CHAPTER EIGHT

EMOTIONAL TRAPS

A lot of teenager trap in this particular topic called emotions, most of them can't control their emotion which causes more pain than ever

EMOTION IN LOVE

It was uncontrollable when it comes to the opposite sex, where people have a romantic mindset,

especially today lot of youngsters are trapped in the matrix of digital media like WhatsApp, Facebook, and Instagram, where they chat with opposite-sex people, for they crave dopamine.

The feeling of love is caused by OXYTOCIN, when you date a girl or when you speak to the girl for too long on a mobile phone or chat with him numerous times, where your oxytocin chemical release in your brain gives you differ feeling

I often see, what a lot of people told me when I give a speech about brain chemicals

They tell, BRO! DID YOU HAVE A LOVE FEELING?

IT WAS AWESOME, WE CAN'T TELL BRO

JUST LOVE A GIRL, FEEL THE PLEASURE BRO!

I often hear this word again and again.....

When you love a girl or share your love with your heart ones, you just notice you behave in an unconscious manner

It was true

When people are in emotional love, where the brain loses its rational thinking level and they go for instant gratification methods

When people chat with their loved ones, when you noticed their faces, there was a lot of excitement, when the message is TYPING, where it will crave the emotion, and suddenly the OXYTOCIN release in your brain, to feel the pleasure...

Some people ask me, SO WHAT CG?

DID YOU HATE LOVE OR LOVE-RELATED THINGS

My answer is NO because I also feel the love and I also love to speak to my heart one's and loved ones

But the problem is

HOW TO MANAGE THE FAILURES

Let's take a brief view

HOW TO MANAGE THE FAILURES

Most people lose their life because of emotional failures, where I not only mention love failures but also friendship betrayals, loss of loved ones, etc

First and most, you should understand, how your brain is wired in the world or how you are wired to see this world,

When you get emotional with your loved ones, where they smile and their facial expression of them and their tone of voice that normally melts your heart and your brain, where you live in an unconscious world[through floating the emotions that surround you]

Initially, everything was good but when any conflict that arises, where you can't understand your loved ones feeling, you feel desperate, the reason is you can't handle your emotions

Man! First understand the emotions that you carried in your life, when your loved ones leave you, don't feel hesitate.

We can't control the environment, but we can control our emotions, when your loved ones leave you, don't be emotional, just through rational analysis,

While in action, just ask the questions like

Where my loved ones leave me, I am in solitude what do I do?

Where your mind tells you, Go to a bar, and drink the wine & reduce the pain, once your spirit tells you that,

I think you can't have an answer to solve this problem

The human brain always blame others for their mistake and they can't accept the mistakes, it was always BLAME BLAME BLAME!

So, once any desperation situation arises, don't react like an emotional guy, Often many of them think suicidal thoughts, where you trained your mind in this type of manner(PLEASE, YOU WANT TO CHANGE YOUR CIRCUMSTANCES, YOU TRAINED YOUR BRAIN AT VERY VERY POOR LEVELS).

MY SPIRIT CHANGED MY DEPRESSION

When on the stage of loss of loved ones, I felt depressed, I can't eat and I feel so tired, I just make diseased.....

But I always tell to myself, I AM SPECIAL, whereas, in this depression, my spirit tells me,

OK! RELAX DUDE!

EVERYTHING OCCURS FOR SOME REASON

JUST ANALYZE AND GET THE KEY

MY spirit specially asked me a question

CG LOOK!

WHERE YOU LOSE YOUR LOVED ONES, DID YOU FEEL SOME PAIN?

I answered, yes! it was heavy pain...

OK, WHERE DO YOU FEEL DEPRESSED FOR THIS PURPOSE RIGHT?

I answered, yes!

CG! LOOK AT YOUR HEART, I ASK ONE THING

A DAY WITH YOUR LOVED ONES

THAT GIVES VALUE OR NOT

I answered, Yeah! It gives value

My spirit again asks,

CG ! NO EMOTIONAL, ONLY RATIONAL THING I WANT

BONDING WITH YOUR LOVED ONES DRIVES MEANING TO YOUR LIFE OR IT WAS A JUST A SHOW-OFF TO BOND WITH THE OPPOSITE SEX?

While answering these questions, I feel something different,

My prime motto is to inspire others to make their dream happen and my goal is TO BECAME THE GREAT ENTREPRENEUR OF SOUTHERN ASIA,

through bonding with the girl, feel some dopamine reactions but it gives value to me, at rational, IT WAS NO

Once I understand these questions, my mind open up a new world for me, to live in, and my depression was suddenly cured and the way of my evolution started something new!

Even if I lose my loved ones, whom I was so happy before with them, my way of life that changes, I love solitude and learning some dead experiences, and working for my lovable dreams.....

THE BOOK THAT CHANGED MY EMOTIONS

During this period, where my mind suggested a lot of books, where one book is HOW TO STOP WORRYING AND START LIVING BY DALE CARNEGIE, a fascinating book, I loved most

Some key points in this book make me think wide, once I feel I AM SPECIAL, as same as D.ale Carnegie tells his book,

Where human life was created by fighting of billion sperms to fuse an ovum, in this competition of billions, where one sperm leads the way to create a destiny, the sperm is you

Fighting billions of sperms in a competition, and winning a victory just feel it was 0.000001% level, very tough competition.

But you win the race and today you read my book, HOW SPECIAL YOU ARE, just imagine man......

So, You feel depressed, where you get to fight across a billion men to get a victory of your precious life......

While I read this book, my mind develops huge maturity, and thank my spirit to lead me on the right path.....

STEVE HARVEY SPEECH MAKES ME SPEECHLESS

Once in a deep depression in my life, due to the betrayal of my friends, I just broke down,

On the day, I searched for some external motivation on youtube, where I get STEVE HARVEY SPEECH,

Where he tells, don't worry about people that the gods removed from your life, because he saw things, you didn't see.

He heard conversations you couldn't hear and he saw he made moves you wouldn't make and that's it!

This speech make me speechless because I often depress about the basics of my emotions, once I hear this speech, my brain pattern of thinking get changed

Yeah! Truly my spirit speaks to me, where I can't hear, see and follow and that's it...

Every occasion I waste my time, my spirit simply tells, me it was time to work hard, not to jollifying, with this understanding of everything, which means people and things that waste my productivity, I erase them from my mind and heart

This gives me huge confidence in my approach that helps me to scale my perception of this world as wide open.

LIFE IS ONE

Life is yours, we only live once in the world,
> don't live for someone else's life
> live your world and live your life for you
> Again FOR YOU!

Through my analysis of this world and maturity of life develops hugely different, I feel something special and erase my irrational thinking and emotional traps

EXTRA FITTING TO GET A WELL LIFE

Once I matured at the top level,

my spirit tells me to follow some habits to change my destiny entirely,

KEY THING I DO

▶ I changed my circle of influence, erased my friends and families, and got grace from my mentors and influencers

▶ I reduced harmful emotions in movies and go for some special motivational thinking

▶ I reduced my voice and listen to the environment, which helps me to think, about how people wired the world

▶ Focusing heavily on my work reduces the time that I spent worriedness and also improves my productivity

Where these keys help me to fit the extraordinary life, that successful people live.

EMOTION IN SEX

I often see most people waste their life in irregular activities, they float their minds with emotion on sex, I think where I recently read a book that shows, that animals have sexual thoughts in seasons, whereas humans have sexual thoughts at any time....

When am I seeing this data, my spirit asks me a question?

WATCHING A ADULT CONTENT THAT REDUCES YOUR PRODUCTIVITY?

I eventually tell, YES

When I have any question in my mind, I just go to QUORA.com, where I see, how people react to these particular questions

Even as a teenager, I find an answer that develops my mindset at a new maturity.

<u>CONSUMER EFFECT</u>

You know, people's lives that react based on the content they consume, where I would be told, when people consume adulterant movies that often expose the emotion of sex in their mind, the HUMAN BRAIN IS REACT BASED ON HOW THE MAN THINKS

When they consume a lot of adulterant movies, their thought process about life is the same as the character they observed in the movies, it caused due to MIRROR NEURONS ON BRAIN

⚙according to the oxford language dictionary

MIRROR NEURONS – Brain cells that react both when a particular action is performed or it will be observed.

Where on the occasion, most people have a huge interest in intercourse, where their conscious thinking was gone mad, which means the RATIONAL THINKING OF THEIR BRAIN IS COLLAPSE

By understanding this theory, I come to the point, where people's habits change their destiny

You may know, a lot of divorces or suicides, commonly occur due to aggression of these emotions

Consuming a high level of this content commonly reduces your creative thinking, where in the worst-case scenario, the brain loses complete control of creativity

Always poses sexual thoughts, that collapse your productivity, often when it comes to focus-related works like meditation, and book reading, on the occasion, your brain acts like a JUMPING MONKEY, that commonly last at sexual thoughts

That imposes you to think again about adulterant movies and your mind carves to get the reward, often you can get control to stop, but the emotional part of your brain that enhances to watch the movie, once you open your phone or laptop, gets to watch, YEAH! Sure your emotions win this match.

I often see, when people tell, where they have sexual thoughts, they go to adulterant sites and consume the content, where the mirror neurons of their brain that poses the same events where they watched, often many singles do masturbation to cure their cravings through the unconscious of their brain.

While finishing the masturbation, they tell, me, where I feel guilty for this purpose, they ask their shadow in the mirror, why did I do it?

This often comes, when people come into the conscious mind, it only occurs when the carve was a cure.

CARVE LEADS GRAVY YARD

When your brain craves you to do something, that is good, when you do productive work but often today smart kids misuse their productive weapons, I mean mobile phones into harmful effects

Even today some 8 to 9 standard have cravings for the emotion of sex, and many of them are suddenly shocked and ask me, HOW CG! HOW A 8 GRADE STUDENT POSES A SEXUAL THOUGHT?

As I previously mentioned, about mirror neurons, where these kids have a smartphone or constantly watching a movie that has some sexual pictures, when one click of their eye lens, hit the sexual thought, BOOM!, Their brain constantly starts cravings but it often occurs at the second and third suggestion of their brains, On this occasion parental control is must for kids to prevent their life.

But effective control fails, when the kids bind with friends that have a craving, this why choosing a friend and partner is so so important in your life to develop something special

Where the peer pressure of these kids, leads to some bad behavior that continues in their future that end with GRAVY YARD.......

HOW TO HANDLE EMOTION IN SEX

Where I can't tell or give a promise, where you can do this or do that may your life can change

But what I suggest is, we can't control emotions, eventually you have sexual thoughts when you see a gorgeous girl, but when the level of this emotion reduces your productivity, you should take care of your thoughts

When it's come to productivity, your number one preference is your goal, because no one comes to you to tell, you want to do that.

Once you develop a work habit or some effective value-driven habits that help you to deviate from these motions

SOME SPECIAL KEYS ARE

▶ Always connect with friends

▶ Reduce sexual thoughts by deviating your thinking to some productivity habits

▶ Measure your cravings and analyze it

For example – when you have a feeling of sexual thoughts commonly at night or on any occasion, notice that where at the breaking point you have a two-choice, yes or no to the cravings, while you analyze your weakness, you will easily know your key points.

<u>EMOTION IN ADDICTIONS</u>

Humans react to their emotions through addictions,

Where is my shop, I see a lot of customers come and buy groceries, and one man comes to my shop, I saw him, he was insane but with perfectionism, through his habit, he constantly buys a cigar and water

I just asked him, what is your problem, and he tells, I have a lot of stress in my workplace. When I get a key, I know his problem.

People always looking for blameless, where they can't accept their failures, always searching for someone to blame

This was the character that passes from generation to generation, I often can't digest this stuff, but it was true.

DOES ADDICTION CURE ILLNESS?

Many people can't take responsibility for their life, when any discomfort arises in their life, they go to a bar or smoke the pain with air, they can't know what their root causes are, but their mind forces them to instant gratification to cure the illness

Most teenagers often affect this trap, sorry! Emotional trap.

Without analyzing the root cause, when the same problems come again, your brain loses the power to interpret the problems, this was the basic insanity where the human generation created the trap.

Once I developed the skill of PROCESS THE ISSUE[i discussed in later chapters], that leads my thinking to a more high level, and enhance my life into something special.

Addiction people often blame others, their life has a lot of problems and pains, once you asked them, they act like a waterfall, which means they pour the thoughts of the world into your ear in a matter of seconds

This type of person doesn't have the emotional maturity, to analyze the situation, that collapses their entire life in a HABIT LOOP.

HOW TO CURE THIS

The simple and most effective method is
ANALYZING THE CHANNEL PATTERNS
In the stock market, where one technical chat pattern is called channel pattern, where the candles travel in the channel, and takes support and resistance along the channel, once they break the resistance, where it indicates bullishness, and as same as it breaks downwards, it indicates bearishness

Why I am telling you this?

By analyzing the patterns, we easily say the market is bull[up] or bear[down]

As same to our thought patterns, once you understand your threshold point and weak point, you understand your strength and weakness and react in that manner.

When you have the plan to quit smoking, it was good for 2 to 3 days, then your brain starts to crave you, on the occasion, any good or bad news comes in your circumstances, your brain that craves you to get a smoke, when you respond this craving, YEAH! YOU ARE ARRESTED

So, to get wonderful value in your life, you should analyze your thought patterns, once you know your craving times, it was better to get avoid this by doing some busy work or something that deviates your mind from these actions.

NOTE – While you deviate your mind from bad actions, you should reward your mind for this purpose. Once your brain understands the patterns, where we prevent these bad actions, we have rewarded, by this analyzing level, you easily recover from this habit....

Yeah! We are in the final part of this topic,

I just remember some golden points

▶Emotion in love is good but when it comes to failure, don't get depressed, just ask your mind whether it gives value to me or not

▶Emotion in sex is also good, good sex leads good life but consuming sexual content that collapse your entire family life and your productivity, analyze and break it

▶Emotion in addictions caused due to lack of understanding of problems, once you check your channel patterns, you easily break it and utilize your energy for some effective habits...

EVOLUTIONARY CHANGES

EVOLUTION IS THE ONLY SKILL THAT DEVELOP YOUR FUTURE AT EXPONENTIAL LEVEL

CHAPTER NINE

HIGH LEVEL THINKING

Once I develop a high-level thinking approach my way of thinking in this world that leads to some special definitions in my life

High-level thinking, which means analyzing the root cause of the problem in the upper level, which means mountain view, on the top level, we easily see the problems and their causes in the bottom

I often mention the term ANALYZE in this section, because that's the only key where we develop a HIGH-LEVEL THINKING

WIDE THINKING

I often focus on a narrow route, because that's the way every kid had to develop in the community, once I see successful people's life, I noticed they have a different domain of knowledge, that they implement in daily activities

You may notice forbes.com's TOP BILLIONAIRE LIST, where most entrepreneurs have a wide range of businesses with different domains, they have this wide range of thinking to scale their business exponentially

For example – ELON MUSK

He had a wide range of thinking, that built his business in different domains[like TESLA, SPACEX, BORING COMPANY, OPEN AI, NEURALINK, etc]

By applying this wide thinking, many ordinary people's life changes into extraordinary...

INVESTOR APPROACH TO WIDE THINKING

You often notice many investors and brokers on the stock market give a piece of advice to a beginner about DIVERSIFICATION

DIVERSIFICATION – in buffet terms, DON'T PUT ALL YOUR EGGS IN SAME BASKET

Because the basket drops, every egg in the basket gets spoiled

What you need to do is diversify the portfolio into many sector stocks

For example – you have the steel sector, auto sector, and IT sector stocks

Suppose the government put a tax on steel, where the steel sector stocks reacted to the market, and start to fall

When your friend has 1000 steel stocks when the stock reacted to fall, think about your friend's situation,........

As same as your situation you have 400 steel stocks and 600 auto and IT stocks, where the news about tax reacted on your steel stocks, were started to fall but 600 auto and IT stocks support your losses, this is why you need to diversify

When you have a wide source of information, your brain easily interprets the issues and quickly makes a decision, suppose you have a weakness in one domain of knowledge, the other domain helps you to support you.

From an entrepreneur's point of view, when you have a wide knowledge that helps to build your business exponentially. when you have weaknesses in any subject, you easily get support from others' strengths.

INFLUENCE OF DAVID EPISTEN

Through some social media influencers, I hear about the book called RANGE BY DAVID EPISTEN, Once I start reading this book, my mindset and way of my thinking totally changed.

People who have a team with different domain knowledge can easily beat the team with the same domain knowledge

For example – you and your college friends start a company related to your subject, on our case, you are a pharmacy graduate, and your partners are too.

When you build your company through a step-by-step process, everything goes well but with some economic policy, your sales are broken down, so what you can do?

As a pharmacy graduate, you only know about your product details, you even not know about cost accounting, inventory shrinkage, EOQ[ECONOMIC ORDER QUANTITY], Cash flow, company sheets, etc

In this situation, everything starts to fall, and your panickiness starts to climb a ladder.

But guess, where you have 3 partners from different domains,

[1] is accountant

[2] one is economist

[3] The guy has +5 years in the business cycle

When any bad situation arises, you easily get the pain points as fast as possible which helps you to view the wide level of your business from your domain partners.

A lot of businesses follow these tactics, where they hire different people with different domain knowledge that helps them to see the wide view, what we called HIGH-LEVEL THINKING

Most people tell me, we are a small business, and we can't have sufficient sources to hire different domain people.

This why I often tell, you should develop a friendship with different domain friends, most college guys have a friend with the same department level, but when you need to start a business, you need to bond with different domain friends, so, only your business scale to next level

But my major request is don't choose your friend to be the partner of your business, without efficient knowledge, everything is sucks! Understand that, Because there is a HUGE DIFFERENCE BETWEEN FRIENDSHIP AND BUSINESS

Don't get mingle your friendship with business,

In simple words,

FRIENDSHIP – emotional and bonding

BUSINESS – strategic and analytical thinking

NARROW VS WIDE

I just want to tell the difference between narrow and wide thinking comparisons, because, we humans, have the skill to compare others to make an effective decision, this was the skill that we develop in the ancient world, and it's totally connected to the emotion section of our brain

Through analyze the difference, we easily get a point

Through analyze the difference,we easily get a point

NARROW	WIDE
FOCUS ON SINGLE DOMAIN	FOCUS ON DIFFERENT DOMAIN
INTERPRET THE INFORMATION AT NORMAL WAY LIKE- CAUSE AND EFFECT	INTERPRET THE INFORMATION AT TOTALLY DIFFERENT VIEW[3D VIEW] LIKE – WHY,HOW,WHAT about cause and their effect
BELIEVE ALL INFORMATION THEY GATHER	ONLY HAVE PROBABILITY APPROACH
FIND EASY WAY TO GET ANSWER	THEY THINK HARD TO FIND A EFFECTIVE ANSWER TO GET A GOOD SOLUTION

NARROW VS WIDE

By seeing this data, you easily understand the difference and make an effective decision

WHY, HOW, AND WHAT APPROACH

Once you make a decision to get a wide view, you must understand WHY, HOW, AND WHAT APPROACH

Most high-level businesses used the FIVE WHY AND FIVE HOW approach to get an answer to the problems, where the company

Every problem occur that comes with these three words

[1] WHY

[2] HOW

[3] WHAT

For example – Your q1 result in 2022 sucked, it was lower than your previous year's record,

By getting this data, a lot of small business owner panics, and their view is totally at narrow level,

Guess what – everything is sucks

But as a high-level thinker, you should ask questions with the effect of three words

[1] why the profit sucks

[2] how our company produce low growth level

[3] what makes our company show a lower growth

When you ask or frame your questions on different scenarios, you easily get an answer

In our case

[1] WHY DOES THE PROFIT SUCK?

Inflation and raw materials hikes affect our profit margin, so, only our profit sucks

[2] HOW DOES OUR COMPANY PRODUCE A LOW GROWTH LEVEL?

Without having prevention like inventory storage, or some warehouse materials, that boil our inventory to trade at a high cost that makes as to reduce our profit

[3] WHAT MAKES OUR COMPANY PRODUCE A LOW GROWTH RATE?

Due to poor management tactics[like different domain team] that shows our balance sheet and cashflow at blood war

By getting this point,

we have a pain point like

[1] inflation + raw material hikes

[2] low warehouse storage or noting

[3] poor management tactics[suppose we have a economist in our team,that guys easily forecast what will

happen in future about commodity and inflation's]

With this point, our wideness will start to operate and it leads to a new way to see the problems.

IMAGINE THE WIDENESS

This topic is so related to movies[especially – thriller movies], where you see the villain group make a crime and use different strategies to fade their identity

The hero of the movie used his wide thinking to interpret the available information to guess the probability one, once they understand the core value, they don't feel they get an answer, because of his wide approach, they always plan to CONNECT THE DOTS

That helps to capture the entire data of the villain group and their alliances

Normal thinking – just go for a crime member

Wide thinker – use to analyze the situation, to get a complete picture of not only the villain group but also track the external links

CONNECTING THE DOTS

When I surfing on youtube, I found Steve Jobs Stanford speech, where he tell about

IMPORTANCE OF TIME

Where his one sentence makes me think over over over over and again

That was

YOU CAN'T CONNECT THE DOTS

LOOKING FORWARD; YOU CAN

ONLY CONNECT THEM LOOKING

BACKWARD.SO YOU HAVE TO

TRUST THAT THE DOTS WILL
SOMEHOW CONNECT IN YOUR
FUTURE
- STEVE JOBS

Once I understand the dept knowledge of connecting the dots skill that literally pays me hugely on the way of my life

When you have different experiences in your life, often you fell

Why god! It was acting on me....

Why do you make my destiny poor manner?

But once you grow to the next level, where you can see the past level in some surprising manner, because it was interlinked with the present, when you get the understanding of connecting dots in a backward way, you easily scale your life into the next level

Because often you see highly successful people have experiences of the past that fuel them to the next level, often it a discussion at an achievement ceremony or TEDx talks

When you have a fear to learn about this stuff, often everything in your life acts as a repeat mode, because everything is a pattern,

Once you play the same pattern a thousand times, where the same thousand answers are available at every turn you made.

If you didn't learn the lesson of the past, everything you create things that have the same error, again and again, your past problems connect to the present answers.

As Beyonce quote,

IF YOU DON'T TAKE THE TIME TO THINK
ABOUT AND ANALYZE YOUR LIFE

YOU'LL NEVER REALIZE ALL OF THE DOTS

THAT ARE ALL CONNECTED

When you see a lot of successful people have a skill of connecting the dots to past to present to future analysis

LEONARDO DA VINCI ALSO MASTER THIS SKILL EFFECTIVELY

LEARN HOW TO SEE

REALIZE THAT

EVERYTHING CONNECTS

TO EVERYTHING ELSE

From ancient philosophers to modern-day CEO have a skill of connecting the dots that help to see the past experience with a wide knowledge to get an effective answer,

Often this was the tactic, that every successful people uses but it was rare to discuss.

CONNECTING THE DOTS THAT LEADS TO

WIDE KNOWLEDGE AND THINKING

THAT HELPS TO PLAY THE COIN

AT EFFECTIVE MANNER

Even in my life, I constantly connect the dots of past experiences to the new beginning of the present,

If I have a pain in my past, whereas in present my mind constantly analyze the situation by connecting the dots that makes wide thinking that helps to see the new world, only a few peoples see this

Once my understanding of connecting the dots improved, I easily see the pain as an opportunity to grow instead of worry or get sorrowful like a narrow thinkers

FOR EXAMPLE – you have a problem with your accounting standards, where your business poses, once you understand the mistakes, it was an easily prevented by a future

By simply, normal your business grows[A], you land at B[PROFIT] but by making mistake, you land at C[ERROR]

by solving the problem,

now you have three dots

A, B, and C

By connecting these three dots to future analysis, you have a better understanding of your business than a man with two dots

Now let's see the most important skill that every entrepreneur has to develop,

PROCESS THE ISSUE, it was a skill

Said by PATRICK BET DAVID[VALUETAINMENT]

PROCESS THE ISSUE

When you have a huge failure or you are in an awful situation, just imagine the scenario, most ordinary people lose their lives in the conditions

If their first business is failed or loved ones have a breakup, most people are in a dead situation, when I ask them, what is the consequences, their replies are literally in a childish manner

They tell, I am going to kill myself or I need suicide, most people act like a child, they didn't develop the skill to sustain the marketplace or human civilization

Process the issue it was a skill that only helps you to think at 4-dimensional approaches

A lot of people get fear of failure or any criticisms that come on their part but our extraordinary man welcomes failures and criticisms because he has the skill to process the issues

So, how to process the issue

Simple by

Get the root causes of the problems, once you understand the root cause, you solved the half problem, then go to the branches

You should ask 5 WHY APPROACH OR 5 HOW APPROACH OR WHY, HOW AND WHAT APPROACH

Once you mastered that, you have a lot of new answers to interpret the problems, which helps you to think in 4 dimensional way

On the occasion, you may think someone's as a genuine guy but when it comes to 4-dimensional analysis, you understand their play

A lot of hidden detail often occurs at 4 dimension

People may tell, I guess the people's character, at initial impression or the type of character they have, but it often misleads because every condition makes people something different, where their characters have a huge change, it was hard to find.

LESSON I LEARNED

One day I am in my father's shop, where small customers come to our shop and buy the necessary things, and I see a man with a small belly, he has a rude character, when he approached me, I was hard-hitting and make a huge temper with me

I guess by his initial impression, where he was a huge drunkard man with a low-paying job

Then I have curious to ask him about the details, and he tell me, he has a job at earns 14000 per day, where he has a transaction of 1.5 lakh every day, I was literally shocked and then I ask him, why are you trapped in the habit loop?

He tells when we earn huge money, our minds start to go for big dreams to get enjoy life, he tells, where high-paying men have a lot of money, their brain goes to entertainment like sex and drugs

Then I understand his causes, he was a high-paying guy but also he have high stress from his job, so he spent 10 to 20 % money on drugs to dissolve his stress and make them pleasure in the next few days.

This understanding leads my thinking to some special things, then I learned, we cannot judge a person's character by his initial impression, with the proper skill of PROCESS THE ISSUE, we master the key!

In simple words

On my occasion, let's think, an ordinary man and a man with the skill of processing the issue

ORDINARY – HE THINKS THAT GUY WAS ARROGANT AND A DRUNKARD

PROCESS THE ISSUE GUY – HIGH PAY MAN WITH HUGE STRESS

By seeing this difference, you literally get the point, YEAH! Once you understand the PROCESS THE ISSUE SKILL, you master the human nature

[note – I often use a soft tone to approach any arrogant man, it makes our conversation huge better, to process the issue

Don't be silly, asking a random question or giving your advice to people, first – you should be a good listener than to be an adviser]

This was the life incident that helps me to see the huge different scenario, only a small class of people see.....

Finish with a quote of mine

If you have to fight the tide

you should ride

with a wide

- CG

In the next section,we see the important life skill that every teenager should learn,

WHAT IS THE SKILL

JUST SEE THE NEXT CHAPTERS.

CHAPTER TEN

SOURCE TO IMPLEMENT TO GET DESIRE ACTION!

I hear a lot of answers that come to people's mind about book reading being a disaster,

A common question about book reading

[1] why do I want to read the book instead of the audiobook?

[2] many successful people don't have the skill of book reading then why do I want to read?

[3] I read a lot of books but my life can't change, so I stop reading.

These are the common questions that people have in their mind

let's see the answer,

[1] this question was good,

According to Leonardo da Vinci, when a human uses his 5 senses to learn a new thing, it takes a short period to complete it, and this way of learning easily creates human evolution at the speed of light

So, using your hearing sense to learn new things that enhance your learning capacity and leads your destiny to fruitful

You may remember, initial stage, I always have a problem to get concentrating on reading, on the time audiobook is the best solution for me to get a new hack.

But there is a huge difference between reading a book and hearing an audiobook

READING THE BOOK	HEARING THE BOOK
IMAGINATION	-
CONCENTRATION LEADS	-

READING VS LISTENING

I often see, a lot of people hearing the audiobook but they lose their concentration when any distraction comes to the path,

Most people often hear audiobooks through driving, walking, running related aerobic exercises but I ask a one question

If you drive a car and hear an audiobook but suddenly a speedy car that crosses your vehicle at top mood, on the time, you will concentrate on the audiobook? NO!, your concentration falls, and you are in a panic situation & thinking about accident scenarios

OR think about this, when you get a jog on public ground, on the way, a gorgeous girl with a pleasant smile crosses across you, At the time, what state of action that your mind have? where does he concentrate on the book or the girl?

This is why often many audiobook followers lose their concentration on their spirit

Hearing an audiobook is good when you are in solitude mood or a silent place, where you have only located this place.

My final answer to this question is,

It depends on how you use [public vs private]

[2] It was an irrational question, In my college days, my friend also tell me, this question.

But most people believe a rule stupidly,

Yeah! In this question, rewrite a word at most to few, because most successful people have a book reading skill in their lifetime, few are exceptional but they have huge experience in their work and they're filed so that helps them to fight the world and win the victory

According to TOM CORLEY's study, where most self-made millionaires have a skill of book reading, In accurate fact, **88%** of successful people have a skill of book reading, they read 30 minutes per day to update their mind

Where some people make a debate, OK! **88 %** read the book but what about 12 %?

Many of them debate and they get well their thoughts but I think, when people tell,12%, often guess this type of guy are lazy, they didn't have the patience to study book, so they spread their gossip to their friends then they start to replicate heavily!

I see my college friends, have a good work ethic but they failed to get approach it because of laziness and they told me, CG! Success does not come from book reading that comes from what you do.

Then I ask a simple question to my friend,

OK! Success has not come from book reading, it comes from actions, I accept that

But how do you get the action?

It is like a develop software without code

When you programmed the code, where did your software start to act but without coding, how did your software act?

In simple terms, humans make actions based on data, where does the data come from?

It comes from experiences when you read a book, you have a whole experience from the author's life, which make an advantage to get to add a mental age of your IQ, which lead to taking effective action in your life

Lots of people didn't have data to possess their actions which cause tremendous stress because without data, how do you get to act?

They tell me I BELIEVE IN MYSELF

OK! That's good because this is also an essential part of success but when it comes to competitive human evolution, your belief in yourself is acting as a photo with a spider net that fixes on a nail in the wood!

Today's world is more competitive than you imagine, in this world, analytical thinking leads to creating your destiny into fruitful, through the point experience that comes from book reading...

In simple words to this question,

WITHOUT DATA, EVERYTHING IS SUCKS!

[3] I frame this chapter in this book, because of this question

I read books but they can't impact my life, so I start quitting, it was the question, right?

Remember our chapter title

SOURCE TO IMPLEMENT

When you read a book, it contains a lot of experiences and knowledge, I often forget some tactics but with consistent effects, it leads to creating a new destiny

Reading a book can change your life but it depends on how you learn this!, you just memorize the words like your school book and prepare for 5 mark question, I'm sorry to tell you, it SUCKS!

The process to implement the experiences with step by step process that leads to creating new learning,

This new learning changes your life with a new way of thinking pattern that causes you to evolve

Most people's common mistakes are

They read a book but without implementing the knowledge source into their life, it is literally like gold in a dust pin scenario.

Often I see a lot of people trapped on this path and blame their circumstances and their communities

Just think about this,

When you are an army general, you learn 100+ war tactics from the book, where written by famous army generals in the decade,

Suddenly, you saw an enemy helicopter in your territory, where you have a tactic formula learned from the book, but you can't know the action plan, on the time, you tell READING SUCKS!

Imagine that, your enemy helicopter shoots a bullet across your territory when one bullet comes nearby your location that suddenly creates a flash of heat with the vibration of land, what is your reaction?

This is why! You should develop a skill that implements THE SOURCE INTO ACTION!

When you know that, I bet you,

You erase this question from entire your life dictionary!

MOTION VS ACTION

There is a huge difference between people who are in motion and people who are in action

MOTION – reading a book

ACTION – applying a book

Once you understand this difference, you easily get a point but the action takes a different approach, we can't interpret motion habits into actions habits

So, only when you read a book, is it good for reading but the same habit can't convert into action!!

You should develop new habits for action-taking...

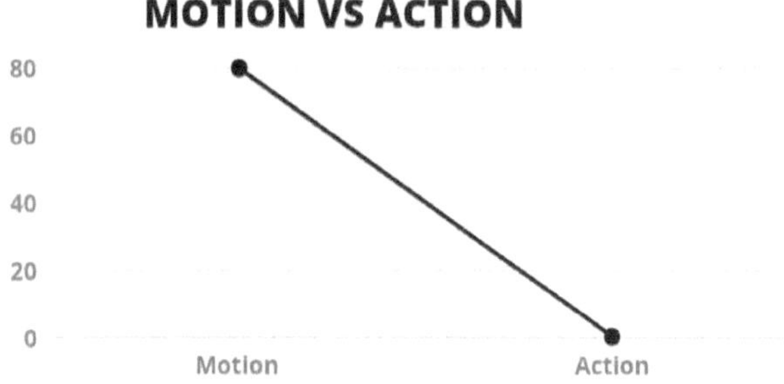

MOTION VS ACTION

When you have 80% of motion, which means knowledge but without action skills capability, it gives only less than 10% results[action]

This is the condition, where every young talent trapped

They tell me, I study hard, I work hard but no results are produced, because of a lack of action-taking skills.

Understanding motion and action lead your life to a different path.

HOW TO IMPLEMENT

This a basic, that every action taker needs to know!

The following 5 steps that help you to get the source and implement it in your life to change your destiny

STEP -1 – GET THE CORRECT DATA

Often most people fail to get correct data from book reading because when it comes to reading a book, we often interpret the experiences with our values or even poor understanding causes a lot, so getting correct data is your main job for implementation

STEP -2 – RESEARCH THE LEADER

When you get the correct data, see the top people on your subject, to get a core belief that helps you to get more confidence in your learning.

STEP -3 GET DIFFERENT KNOWLEDGE

I often use these tactics in my learning, when I finished steps -1 and step -2

I go to youtube and search for the related topics, I want to learn, and on the first page, it has the top 1 to 8 videos, I often see 10 videos[on the top list], and it helps me to see different people point of view on same subjects, that help my critical thinking into the new zone!

STEP -4 HABIT FORMING

By getting the source of knowledge, you can feel self-confident in your approach but without an action plan ......

So, you must develop the habit of implementation with tactics[I explain in latter chapters]

STEP -5 COMPOUNDING

Once you insert the source to implement, you feel a lot of internal change in your life, but a single change can't impact much, so you should develop at COMPOUND EFFECT

Like sip investment, you should invest your source to implement funds to get the benefit of compound interest, by constantly upgrading yourself into the new path with a compound effect, I bet you, you will make a huge impact in your life.

These are the five steps that help you to convert

SOURCE TO IMPLEMENT.

<u>YOUR ACTION PLAN</u>

Your action plan must give your investment effective returns

This means you should divide your time into four quadrants, I refer to some self-help books

[1] urgent, important

[2] important but not urgent

[3] urgent but not important

[4] no urgent and no important

I explain this topic in detail,

[1] URGENT AND IMPORTANT

Urgent is the word derives the meaning, this was the work, you need to do, and importantly represents the value of your investment in your life

When you make a habit formation, your action plan should be on this approach,

Because of constant research, we get a lot of data but without the skill of filtering out, it's like a river with fresh and drainage water.

So filter out Urgent and important things in your schedule, that makes you get a clear idea of your action plan.

Often you get a ton of data, and when you tell your brain to implement action, Your brain repairs!

But through the filter out urgent and important things, you get a minimum amount of data, to get implement

That makes your brain more confident in action!!

[2] *IMPORTANT AND NOT URGENT*

During my teen years, I have often stuck with these problems,

At this time, I can't develop the skill, to get see the difference between important and urgent things

I just constantly work hard on data, I even can't bother about important and urgent things, I just invest my time in the subjects.

But guess what?

It sucks!

Then I realize,

Working hard on the wrong path

Can't make you turn a right ladder

Then, I realize, workaholic behavior is good but the wrong path leads to destroying the results and your time

Then I start to differ, which is urgent and which is important

Important things are a must but it was not necessary to do today or the following week, so you should delegate the work or do it in future periods.

It was a wonderful skill, that successful man want's to know!

[3] URGENT BUT NOT IMPORTANT

A little bit confusing with [2] and [3] right?

Urgent means need to be done at the right period but important is done[not need to done]

On this occasion, where things that have urgent and important are given priority, then the urgent and not important

I usually delegate this work to my team members, that solves the urgency and the not important one

In business, you do OUTSOURCING for this act, it solves your problems and makes you do the work more effectively.

[4] NOT URGENT AND NOT IMPORTANT

When your major priority on [4],

I am sorry to tell you,

You waste your valuable time

I see a lot of ordinary people do these mistakes

They don't recognize it, and it was a painful act I ever see

Wasting your time, with 0 return on investment, it's like a buy a diamond Diller to capture 1g of gold.

It was a waste of time and reduce your productivity

so, avoid it.

I just want to highlight this point, because my friends and partners are often trapped on this [4]

so in bold lines,

NOT URGENT AND NOT IMPORTANT – AVOID IT

When you get to the point, your actions start to count!

SKILL TO MASTER

When I read a lot of books, I get enough knowledge to sustain human evolution but comes to reality, everything is a source, my brain was still empty, and it can't automate the decision, what I read in a book

It was a hard thing, where my brain thinks

one simple example – I read more than 4 books about financial statements and their details

When I see an original balance sheet in my hand, my brain was empty, I struggle a lot to recap my learning but it fail's

By facing constant struggles, where my brain starts to get data from the source, that helps to evolve my life into exponential

Focusing a lot of data cause your brain tremendous stress, so step by step process that leads to getting a gem

Let's say you have a book to become a billionaire, which contains 1500 pages

When you start reading a book, where your curious sense an increase, after reading 2 to 5 pages, suddenly a falling ball effect has occurred

FALLING BALL EFFECT

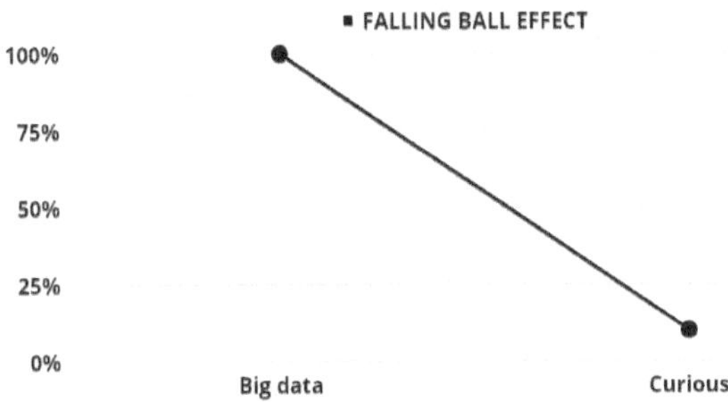

FALLING BALL EFFECT

[falling ball effect means where your focus and curious start to decrease because of abundant data]

then your journey to becoming a billionaire is a like a dream that a kid has.

OR let's say you have 12 steps to become a billionaire, all the steps that are printed on a single piece of paper

On-time you have BULLET EFFECT in your brain because it was a single paper data, so you think it was so easy to follow,

[BULLET EFFECT – means like a bullet, where your curiosity increase and fire at a particular target[your dream]]

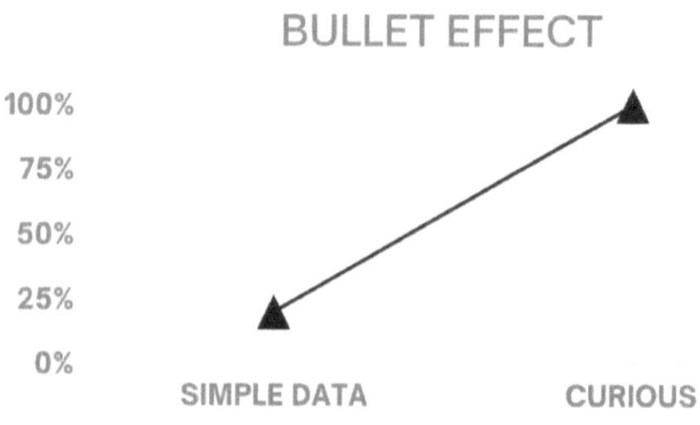

BULLET EFFECT

This was a simple way to recognize your source to implement the data

You should take a summary of your reading in a single paper with simple steps that help you to recognize the data and it was easy to implement in your life.

STRUGGLE PHASE

When you first start your journey on the source to implement, it was hard at first, you struggle more and more than ever before

Because your mind was initially in the storage phase, which means collecting the data but implementing was different, So it takes an act of huge courage to do the process, but once you develop the skill to get implement, it was so easy to learn even hard things at easy ways.

GET HELP FROM MENTORS

By journeying on the struggling phase, you are so depressed, so always go with the mentors, where those people who already phase the resistance or if you didn't find any mentors

MM! NOWAY, you can do it yourself because it was a right way

But some guys recommend taking advice from teachers,.........I didn't want to tell anything

Because most people even didn't understand the difference between mentors and teachers

When you see that, it changes your perception of the world

Let's see the difference

MENTORS	TEACHERS
They tell experiences	They tell theories
They live their dream life and share their life struggles & pleasures to others	They live in different life and tell the stories that literally different phase of their life
They inspire people to take action	They teach people to take action
They focus on value	They focus on marks
Mentors make the followers,mistakes to learn	Teachers punish the students when the mistake is made
Mentors love co-operation[team]	Teachers love solo[because co-operation is illegal to school test rules]

MENTORS VS TEACHERS

We make a huge difference in this comparison, but it's not my purpose

My goal is to get to know the value that the mentors provide,

I see a lot of successful people in their initial stage have a mentor in their life because these guys make an initial push to the young entrepreneur to get sustained in the marketplace.

SOME POWERFUL MODELS DEVELOP A SKILL TO IMPLEMENT THE SOURCE TO GET A DESIRABLE ACTION

MODEL -1 VISUAL PROCESS BY YOURSELF

FLOW CHART OF VISUAL PROCESS

VISUAL PROCESS

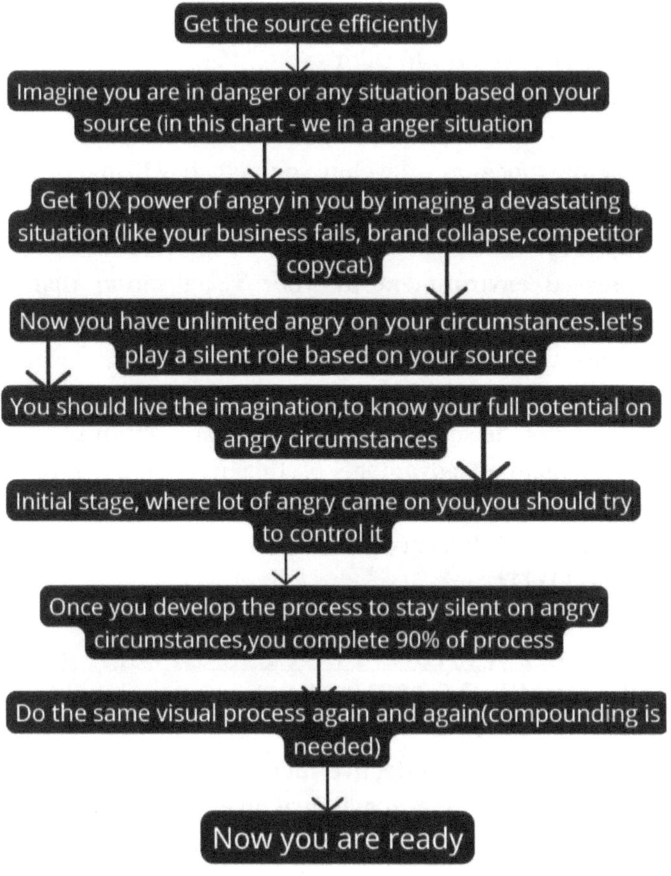

VISUAL PROCESS

In this process, you visualize your source data, If you have a source to stay calm on depress situation,

What do you do?

This was key, Just imagine yourself, you are in a depressing situation, and you have a lot of anger to express, but you try to calm's you

By making this imagination, act you check the capability where you have in yourself, initially, it was crazy but once you develop yourself, it will pay off in future

Because when you train yourself to calm down in a depressed environment by your visualization that is mirrored in your reality.

Once you understand this process, where automatically your brain interprets the data and implements the source to get the desirable actions

The main disadvantage of this method is it often depends on your capability, where you have poor skills and capacity, it hurts you more than you think

NOTED IT!

MODEL-2 VISUAL PROCESS BY LEADERS OR MODEL OF MIRRORS

It was the most effective method when it's come to implementing source-to-action at an exponential level

It works from the power of mirror neurons, once you have a collective power of mirroring, you easily get a desirable action

Here's the flow chart

VISUAL PROCESS BY LEADERS

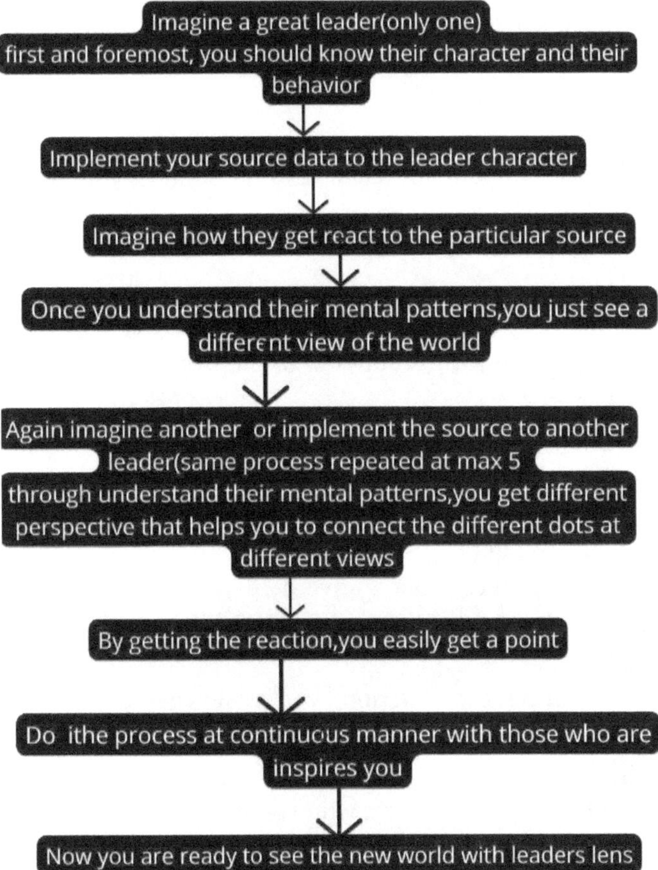

VISUAL PROCESS BY LEADERS

The visual process of leaders that are formed by the following eight steps

<u>STEP -1</u>

Imagine a great leader

First and foremost, you should know their character and their behavior

<u>STEP -2</u>

Implement your source data to the leader's character

<u>STEP -3</u>

Imagine how they get react

<u>STEP -4</u>

Once you understand their mental patterns

You just see a different view of the world

<u>STEP -5</u>

Again imagine another great leader, repeat the steps, max up to 5 leaders

Once you understand their entire mental patterns

Yeah! You get it!

[Often, different perceptive helps you to connect the different dots at the different location]

<u>STEP -6</u>

By getting the reaction, you easily get a point of difference

<u>STEP -7</u>

Do it consistently with, who you inspire a lot

<u>STEP -8</u>

Now, you have the power to see, how your leader thinks about the particular situation or how your leader gets to react on your source

<u>FOR EXAMPLE</u>

If your source is 'CALM' on the abundant situation[bulk amount of cash]

Remember, step number 1, Imagine a great leader or the guy who inspires you.

Ok! I write my inspirations

▶ELON MUSK

▶STEVE JOBS

▶JACK MA

▶WARREN BUFFET

▶MARCUS AURELIUS

If am in this situation[abundant money], without having a mindset to tackle the abundant, It ruined my life.

Let's see through the details

When you have abundant money in your hands, you are the number 1 person in the world, who own billions and billions of dollars

At the time, what did you do?

Many peoples go to spend their money on sex and drugs.

Just think, how my inspirations tackle this situation, it was based on my thinking[it depends on how I collect this data]

[1] ELON MUSK

I think he replies to this question on his Twitter,

When people on Twitter, tweet Elon musk, you are the number -1 billionaire in the world,

But his reply is LET'S DO OUR WORK

These words show his maturity and how they understand their world.

[2] STEVE JOBS

When you read his biography, you easily guess, what is his reply.

`Steve jobs didn't have a dream of abundant or he didn't interest in money[even tons] because his focus totally on value creation In the world

This way he is known as

THINK DIFFERENT.

[3] JACK MA

Jack ma is the leading giant in Chinese corporates

He failed at countless and bankrupt & collapse his business in the early days of his life

But yeah! Today history speaks....

Once you ask him about this abundance question, I think he replies with a calm tone and thinks about his further business expansion worldwide.

[4] WARREN BUFFET

No words, calm, and just invest.

[5] MARCUS AURELIUS

According to stoic philosophy, we eventually dead at one time, so you have abundant money, to think to enjoy,

Just Imagine, the difference between the death of tomorrow and the next 50 years

In this universe, it was a micro level

Think praise and help others to your abundant wealth, to create a history[fruit] in your life

By analyzing my inspirations, you shocked!

Because no one thinks to enjoy their life with drugs and sex etc

Due to one thing,

THEY HAVE A PURPOSE IN THEIR LIFE

When you read, MAN SEARCHING FOR MEANING BOOK BY VICTOR FRANKLIN, you get a point about what successful people tell about 'PURPOSE'

So, once you understand successful people's perceptive, it was easy to see the world with a different lens, often it is only seen by 0.0001% of the world

This method was more effective than the first one, MODEL-1[You think about yourself] but MODEL-2[where you think about successful people, so it creates a different dot, rarely seen by people]

Understand this model and implement your life, definitely your life start to change !!

MODEL -3 MOVES THE MIND

In this method, we apply the visual process to different people's approaches and views, to get a quick insight into how people react to a particular source of data, which helps to implement the data to action at an exponential level

(But note – model -1 and model -2 are tells, a visual process of you and one particular person, but model -3 is a particular circumstance of people).

I didn't recommend this method, because it often works against you,

In this model, I recommend circumstances.

Imagine circumstances have only 0.001% of successful people and 20 to 30 % of good loving people but more than 70 % are in danger

[I amn't mean thieves or corruption, I mean people without purpose, without purpose, they are also dangerous, for people who have a purpose!

So, circumstances often lead fallacy environment

Beware of this model, again I OFTEN DIDN'T RECOMMEND MODEL TO ANYONE

Once you gather the data from unsuccessful people, where people without purpose, often leads to disaster effect

This causes you some pain or misinformation, because, humans are like a chameleon, they can't expose the same action again, but once you understand their character, it was better to take an insight]

It was a hard process but an effective one, like an investor searching for stocks, you should search a people

This means, your source has to react with a variety of people

Let me explain in detail,

Once you get a source, then apply the process of thoughts to different people

Just say, you have a source to get silent when anger comes into your life,

By developing this model,

You just moved your mind though[silent] to your fellow human beings

Like how did your father react to anger?

How did your mother react to anger?

How does your brother or sister react to anger?

How does your girlfriend or spouse react to anger?

Imagine the source to apply with different people, you are surprised, by how people react to angry situations.

These insights help you to break the blind spots and constantly help you to apply the source

When you just have a source to be silent, where you can't know the circumstances of people, you are in the trap.

For example – you and your dad are in a pleasant place, and suddenly a stressful and angry situation raises a high, where you prefer silence but when your dad shouted like a storm, to release his anger, often you also react, because this was the theory of mirror neurons

When knowing your circumstances very well, you easily get an insight, into where your father reacts like, when the angry situation comes on, once you know that, you easily control yourself and apply the source of your silence to get a desirable result.

In business terms,

Let's imagine you are in 10 core debt traps,

Imagine you have a plan to recover the debt from some source like selling a patent product

Where you imagine

How father reacted to this debt trap? What does he do?

How do brothers or family react?

How do competitors react?

How management reacts?

How do mentors react?

Once you have a different point of view of circumstance, you easily get to know how people react to this specific source,

Master this art, you easily know other people's views which helps you to apply the source at an exponential level

These are some interesting models that help you to get the source applied to get action, NO! DESIRABLE ACTION.

CHAPTER ELEVEN

DETERMINATION PATH FORMULA'S

What is the formula?

The formula is the rule that helps to solve a particular problem in everyday life

Determination path – the path that was chosen by highly successful people, to create value in their life

When knowing the determination path formulas that help you to achieve an exponential manner

Is like a mathematical formula, once you have a formula in your hands, it was easy to solve the problem in a matter of seconds instead of thinking a lot hours

In my life, I see a lot of experiences and hear a variety of pain stories from many many peoples, along with this experience, I create six formulas, where every human need to know this, NO!

Need to master this !!

CREATING A FORMULA TAKES TIME

BUT FOLLOWING A FORMULA IS EASY!

[1] SUCCESS FORMULA

$$S = PE + SE \times M$$

S = SUCCESS
PE = PERSONAL EXPERIENCES
SE = SOURCE OF EXPERIENCES
M = MATURITY LEVEL

When you need success, you should have to learn from your personal experiences and add your source experiences[which means the book you read, the inspiration you follow, etc] and multiply your maturity levels

My personal experiences come, from people I met, and people I love a lot,

when you love a person, suddenly his or her character is exposed, maybe he or she doing dishonest with your approach, which makes you break this relationship, Suddenly pain and isolation come on our track. My thinking patterns were changed and go to death end & depressed. Then through your spirit power, you constantly recover from this incident.

There were examples of personal experience
and,

Once you get developed an attitude to get approach highly emotional things with your source of experiences, where you get succeed

Let me explain

When you do a business, the initial stage it was awesome but a period comes, when no cash comes to your treasury which means neutral cash flow, on that time, everyone thinks, of depression attitude, and a golden question comes to their mind.

WHY DID I START A BUSINESS?

MY DAD TOLD, DOING BUSINESS IS HARD BUT I DO, TODAY[at cry emotion, just read a question again]

This was the reality, where every one phase and that leads their maturity level into collapse

On this occasion, you need +[additional factor], which means source experiences[generally, I refer to MENTORS]

Those guys help you, when you are in the downward, the way of attitude a mentor, enhances our performance & attitude into the next level

When you have your personal experience with a spirit and source experience with a will that gets stable with your maturity levels, the whole formula leads you to get succeed.

This was the lesson, I learned from my life when I get a depressing feeling, my spirit gives a positive vibration to recover from the situation but needs some external stimuli to get well, so I find a source experiences from motivational videos and from my books that help my insights to stronger. My maturity level in the circumstances leads me to get a fruit, so-called SUCCESS.

[2] PAIN SOLVING FORMULA

P = E / L
Meaning,
P = PAIN
E = EMOTIONS
L = LESSONS
' In the denominator of this formula, you see, which means LESSON

[Simple rule for a denominator is, have the power to reduce the numerator value]

When you have powerful lessons in your life that helps you to divide or reduce the painful emotion that occurs in your life, that leads you to recover at a fast and exponential

For example – When my loved ones break my relationship dishonestly, I get emotions and feel the pain at the first factor of my life, I can't explain this in words, because,......Yeah! So much.....

But my life lessons, and my purpose, woke me at the early swallow of pain, and my books[especially – HOW TO STOP WORRYING AND START LIVING] that book change my perspectives on emotions, When I learned these life lessons, my life changed!

So, always remember, once you have pain in your life, get along with the lesson that teaches you to reduce the emotion instantly, which helps you to see a different view of your life.

[3] PROBLEM-SOLVING FORMULA

P = [AL x CS]n
Meaning,
P = PROBLEM
AL = ANALYTICAL
CS = CORRECT SOURCE
n = number of times multiples
Did you know, HOW PROBLEM RAISE?

Problem raise due to unknown factors, which means like a circle of ants, when one ant breaks the pattern, due to any external sense, where the circle change, in a matter of seconds, the entire circle is collapse

Same with problems, when you have a good tone of action, when any external factor influence you, that breaks your action and makes your productivity into a depressed path

By facing these problems, you just need an analytical skill that helps you to see the problem at a 360-degree angle

Like connecting the dots, you should connect your problems with your circumstance.

On this path, you need a correct source, because a wrong source can lead to the biggest trap that you have ever seen.

So, always get the correct source from the correct people, when you developed the analytical skill with the correct source, you can multiply it the number of times, by your efficient analysis, which helps to solve the problem in a matter of seconds.

For example – When I develop a new product that is related to weight loss, and I get failed due to the stability of my product preparation, I get depressed but through analysis of my product, I understand it's due to incompatibility, then I ask my teacher[CORRECT SOURCE] and internet surfing, I get an insight, that helps to solve the problems, with the victory of several products I made.

[4] FORMULA FOR STRENGTH

S = T + C -D
Meaning,
S = STRENGTH
T = TRUST
C = COMMITMENT
D = DISHONEST
When you speak about strength, you can't avoid this topic, it was TRUST

One of the effective formulas, that can make your life so pleasant

Trust and commitment are the first-factor sources of strength, especially in team strength and less dishonesty

A good example is OUR FREEDOM FIGHTERS

The team strength of their groups with the trust and commitment of every soldier that leads our India strength into the next level, with less dishonesty in this act, makes our strength exponential manner

That strength feels every soldier's heart and they live with it to the last second of a republic.

[5] EGO CAUSING FORMULA

$E = - A - SE$

Meaning,

$E = EGO$

$A = ANGER$

$SE = SELF ESTEEM$

You see, where we put numbers on this formula that cause NEGATIVE RESULT, Which means CAUTION

The ego is the worst enemy I encounter, through these harmful circumstances, we face a lot of people with a lot of characters, When you start to compare yourself to others that lead to a starting point of problems, and the EGO derives every wrong path, you have ever seen in your life.

Anger[negative], eventually the worst enemy, make you unconscious, where your emotions[amygdala] hijack your entire actions. read........

High negative anger leads your self-esteem to a lower level, Which makes your power in your circumstance a negative manner[Always note it]

When your self-esteem is low, peoples disrespect you that cause you mental illness, even small ones who tease you because of only one content is EGO

So, getting the insights in this formula leads to you preventing any negative situation that you face in the future.

[6] HAPPINESS FORMULA

H = I -E

Meaning,

H = HAPPINESS

I = INTERNAL

E = EXTERNAL

Happiness is come from within, once you understand this formula, you can't search for your happiness in external sources or peoples

You see this formula,

I – E

Like at GDP formula [X-M]

This means EXPORTS[X] – IMPORTS[M], when your exports raise more than your imports, you made a good amount of foreign exchange, when your IMPORTS raise more than your exports, that reduces your foreign exchange level, which causes a trade deficit.

as same as in happiness,

INTERNAL – EXTERNAL, when you have your happiness in your inner self than your external circumstances, I bet you!

You're the happiest person in the world

For example – In my life, I always pass my happiness in my external circumstance[friends, or any things, foods] but once my friend breaks my trust or my favorite food miss in demand, I feel depressed. But through my analysis of the world, I am grateful for what I have, I just follow Gratitude principles, which leads to my happiness in my inner self than external

Today, my friends are not with me, but I was happier than before Because I found the secret formula to happiness.

Every day, I expect something for my loved ones, Guess what ?, it always causes me, pain and make me unhappy but once I understand the formula, the reduce my expectation of my friends and still enjoy the happy mode when my friend does not come to my expectation.'

Ancient peoples get well understand this formula, according to stoic philosophy the term happiness that comes from within

Through the famous Marcus Aurelius quote

'VERY LITTLE IS NEEDED TO MAKE A HAPPY LIFE;

IT IS ALL WITHIN YOURSELF.

IN YOUR WAY OF THINKING

Dale Carnegie also proposed internal happiness, in his writings

'BEGIN HAPPY DOESN'T DEPEND ON

ANY EXTERNAL CONDITION,

IT IS GOVERNED BY OUR MENTAL ATTITUDE'

A PATH OF DETERMINATION

Once you get understand these six formulas. You can easily tackle the life problems that come to your life. Because humans mislead their life due to lack of information, they can't develop the skill to understand their lackness, and they still worry about their problems

But once you get a formula for every problem, it was easy to apply to your life, you can start to see the changes at the initial changes of your life!

Determination is not easy when you have a lack of information, so minded it!

To Tommy Lasorda quote,

'THE DIFFERENCE BETWEEN THE IMPOSSIBLE AND

THE POSSIBLE LIES IN A

A PERSON'S DETERMINATION'

Without sufficient data in our hands, we may tell IT WAS IMPOSSIBLE but by analyzing the situation, it was easy than we think through lack of information and ignorance cause these problems

Good data always enhance our determination to the next level which leads to our success at mountain high.

MY LIFE MODELS

CHAPTER TWELVE

HABIT MODELS

A famous quote from BRAIN TRACY

SUCCESSFUL PEOPLE ARE SIMPLY THOSE WITH SUCCESSFUL HABITS

You may also see that quote from JOHN C.MAXWELL

YOU'LL NEVER CHANGE YOUR LIFE UNTIL YOU CHANGE SOMETHING YOU DO DAILY. THE SECRET TO YOUR SUCCESS IS FOUND IN YOUR DAILY ROUTINE

A HABIT LOOP

When I read the power of habits book from Charles dughigg, I get info on how habits really work in human evolution

By doing the same thing again and again, we lose our rational thinking and enter into a routine.

Habits are good or bad, it depends on, how you use them!

Developing a skill set into constant motion of doing again and again literally pays off in the long term

But non-productive things literally ruin your entire life, you don't even know the fallacy, because you turn this insight into habits

Imagine you drink tea at morning 7 AM, afternoon at 2 PM, and evening at 6 PM, when this time comes on your watch, your brain starts to think the pattern, to want to drink a tea

This was a loop

Tea is not a big stuff

But the world of people literally trapped their entire life in this habit loop

Let's see some economical data

Important note – When I set a chapter in my book that related to HABITS, most people think it was self-help, but my point of view is different when it comes to habit modeling,

Where we can easily write a book about HABITS, like just a follow one thing, doing it consistently with discipline, it develops a habit

Yeah! Every self-help book frames its topic on this type

But when it comes to an economic and psychological analysis of people's behavior, you literally see a big difference in people's lives based on their habits

Habits often followed by unconscious nature, once you developed, it was hard to break, lets the see example of inheritance data

HABIT OF SAVING

When you ask about a new thing or new product, it cost more than your parent's budget, their replies often come to save money to get the product. It was an ancient process, that develops from generation to generation to follow the habit of saving to achieve your dreams

In my childhood years, the same event occurs, where I ask a new cricket bat to my father, and he tell me to save money to get my dream bat, then my habit of saving started......

Whenever I want anything, I go through the process of saving, to increase my hand cash and reduce & sacrifice my expenses and short-term desires

THE HABIT OF SAVING IS A WONDERFUL TOOL TO GET THE DESIRES IN LONG TERM VIEW

But a lot of people confuse saving and investment same, I see many grannies tell their savings are their investments, but often it causes a disastrous effect

Because of a lack of knowledge in economical terms like INFLATION, STAGNATION, etc

New to thing topic, let me explain

INFLATION

According to International Monetary Fund[IMF] defines inflation – it measures how much more expensive a set of goods and services has become over a certain period, usually a year

In simple words, when you buy a biscuit at ?5 [containing 60gram] in 2021, whereas the same biscuit at ?5[you get only 40gram] in 2022,it was known as inflation

HOW INFLATION OCCUR

It occurs for a variety of reasons like

▶PRODUCTION COST INCREASES[it occur due to raw materials price increases,it often occur by supply and demand theory]

▶CURRENCY DEVALUTION[When dollar strengthens,it directly affect the purchasing power of money]

▶MONEY SUPPLY[as same supply and demand theory,when government print more money that exceeds supply,that cause inflation]

▶POLICIES AND REGULATION[Best example was SRI LANKA,where government put the policies to shift to organic farming methods,that cause shortage of raw material,that get impacted on huge price increases,it leads inflation]

According to the Sri Lankan government, where In January to February data, contains inflation of about 10 -20 %, whereas in June it cross more than 50 %[approx 54.6%], when you buy a packet of milk at 10 Sri Lankan rupee[200ml], the same milk packet rate sky rocked 50% from the original one, which means 15 Sri Lankan rupees for same 200ml milk.

This was the main concern.

The average inflation rate of India is 5.13% but in march 2022, India's inflation is 6.95% and in June 2022, it shows 7.01%

Food inflation in india crosses 7%[approx 7.75% on 2022,where it from 3.7% on 2021]

Let's show some important data about India's Inflation

INDIA	
INFLATION RATE	
HISTORICAL DATA	
YEAR	INFLATION RATE
1960	1.78%
1970	5.09%
1980	11.35%
1990	8.97%
2000	4.01%
2010	11.99%
2015	4.91%
2020	6.62%
2021	5.13%
2022[TILL JUNE 2022]	7.01%

INFLATION RATES IN INDIA

When you see the chart, you understand the flow of inflation in India from 1960 to 2022. Different times when inflation hikes and downs, it occurs due to a lot of reasons that followed by particular periods

When inflation peaks, the habit of saving is collapses NOTED AGAIN THE WORDS

WHEN INFLATION IS HIGH, THE PURCHASING POWER OF THE RUPEE FALLS, SO THE PEOPLE WHO SAVE THEIR MONEY ON THEIR HOMES START TO LOSE THE VALUE.

STAGNATION

[ANOTHER BIGGEST VILLAIN]

According to Robinhood traders, where stagnation occurs when the size of an economy remains the same or no growth will happen.

When the economic growth of the country was under 2 to 3 % level, it was considered a stagnant country

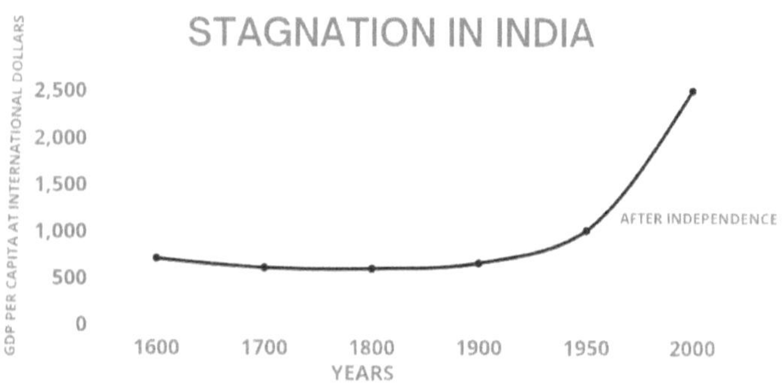

STAGNATION

For example – India before independence, shows a huge stagnation in growth, it was due to some irregular policies of the British government on india[in simple terms – the British invested money in railways but not in irrigation, so the agricultural output of India start to decline and industries on this period only employed 10% of this workforce, that cause huge stagnation in India.

But it lateral recovered after the independence of India.

Let's see the two giants in a single image

Which means

STAGFLATION

Which means stagnation + inflation

It occurs due to three factors

▶ SLOW ECONOMIC GROWTH

▶ INCREASE INFLATION

▶ INCREASE UNEMPLOYMENT

Some root causes of stagflation

▶ Shortage of goods and services

▶ poor fiscal and monetary policies

[technical term – MONETARY POLICY

the policy conducted by the reserve bank of India, to control the money supply in an economy]

Stagflation occurs during the 1970s oil crisis, due to a shortage of crude oil that cause slow growth in the world economy

In 2021-2022, the world economy faces the COVID-19 pandemic and Russia -Ukraine war that collapse the entire supply chain, where it results in the growth rate slowing from 5.7% to 2.9% on 2022

That causes a lower risk of stagflation in India.

By seeing this economic jargon, you get a point about inflation and stagnation

Let's see the habit of saving vs inflation

First, see the saving account interest rates of top banks in India

SAVING ACCOUNT INTEREST RATES	
BANK	**INTEREST RATE[BELOW RS.1 LAKH]**
AXIS BANK	3 %
HDFC BANK	3%
ICICI BANK	3%
KOTAK MAHINDRA BANK	3.50%
STATE BANK OF INDIA	2.70%
INDUSIND BANK	3.50%
BANK OF BARODA	2.75 %
CANARA BANK	2.90%
YES BANK	4%

Just average, and imagine we have a 3% saving interest in the bank

Compare with inflation data

In 2022 – India has 7% inflation data

In 2022 – our saving rate is 3 %

Just calculate the results

3% - 7% = - 4%

negative returns

when you deposit 100 rupees in your saving account at 3% interest, you made 103 rupees per year but inflation is 7%, so [-7 rupee on your 103 rupee gain, which comes to 96 rupees, where you lose[-4 rupee or 4% of your principle capital]

This is why I explain inflation and stagnation in this topic

and this is why SAVERS ARE LOSERS

HABIT OF BRAINWASH

Without this above information, you can't get wealthy. But most people[especially the middle class and poor people save their money and think they do intelligent work, but it fails once you understand the concepts

But the middle class and poor people families were trapped in the mental patterns to save and get rich, it was a fallacy and they get down from generation to generation that creates tremendous failure in future

When I ask my friend about investing and saving, he has no answer to tell, because he is also trapped in this brainwashed habit followed by his parents

Some surveys tell the truth about Indians and financial management

According to national statistical office[NSO] data,2021,

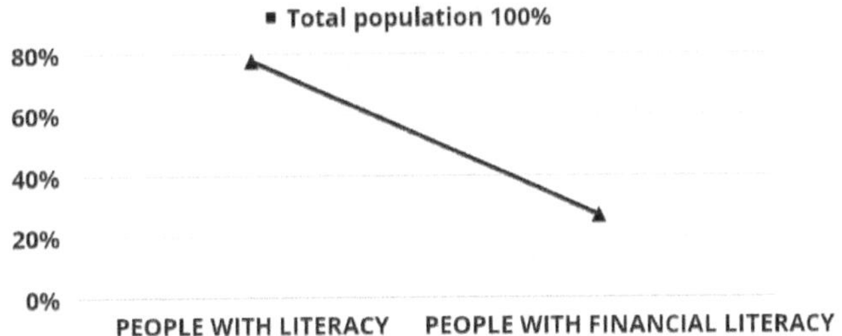

LITERACY VS FINANCIAL LITERACY

Indian average literacy rate is 77.70%

male literacy at **84.70%**

female literacy at **70.30%**

As per SEBI[SECURITY EXCHANGE BOARD OF INDIA], only **27%** of the country's population is financially literate compared to **57%** in the united states

and only **24%** of millennials demonstrate basic financial literacy

Compare the data, where India has high literacy in traditional education but only **27%** in financial education

FALLING OF FQ

What is FQ?

FQ – means FINANCIAL QUOTIENT

Put in the formula

FQ = WEALTH OBTAIN

MONEY MANAGEMENT

Why money management in the denominator, because the denominator has the power to reduce the numerator values[even at 0]

This means poor money management skills lead to a decrease in the entire wealth you obtained in the years

So, only I put on the denominator!

For example – a famous doctor lived in a town, made 10,000 per day, and live an upper-middle-class level of life, after his expenses in his job, he make 2 lakh per month.

It was literally good! People who need to live a better life. So, only many parents force their sons/daughters to MBBS[even my parents]

But the truth is even a doctor can make 2 lakh per month, without money management skills, which ruins

Suppose the doctor buys a car, home furniture, and other accessories

These purchases make him a debt of 3 lakhs per month and he can't bear these expenses that make his investment at a poor level, because of a lack of money management skills

lets the FQ of the doctor

FQ = 2 LAKH[WEALTH OBTAIN]

3 LAKH[MONEY MANAGEMENT]

= 0.66[it was poor]

So, only I tell you what job you are doing is not a matter, it's how you manage it, it's a real matter

In Robert Kiyosaki's tone,

It's not how much money you make, but

how much money do you keep,

how hard it works for you, and how many

generations you keep it for.

Again one example – where you are a laborer in small industries, it gives 10,000 rupees per month as a salary

you know very well about money management tactics, you save money and invest in index funds, that make 12% returns annually and you sacrifice for an instant gratification approach that helps to see what is needed at this time and what type of things we need to expand our lives.

Let's say

1 month's salary – 10,000 rupees

1-year salary – 1,20,000 rupees

He invests his amount at index funds[10% of his salary -which means 12,000] annually

He spent 90,000 per year on his expenses and utilities

On 1,20,000 – he invest 12,000 + his expenses 90,000
total amount = 1,02,000
and the remaining 18,000, he separates into three parts

▶ 6,000 for the trip, entertainment purposes

▶ 6,000 for an emergency fund

▶ 6,000 was invested in gold and pieces of jewelry
With this allocation,
After 20 consecutive years,
His index funds alone make him a 7.5 lakh profit
[1,000 monthly sips, by the year it went on 12,000 rupees
at 20 years, he invested 2,40,000 in index funds
That makes an estimated return of 12%[is 7,59,148 rupees]
And his gold investment also makes him good returns
According to some resources,

GOLD RETURNS	
YEARS	CAGR
15 YEARS	11.6%
20 YEARS	12.4%
25 YEARS	9.4%

In graph,

GOLD RETURNS IN INDIA

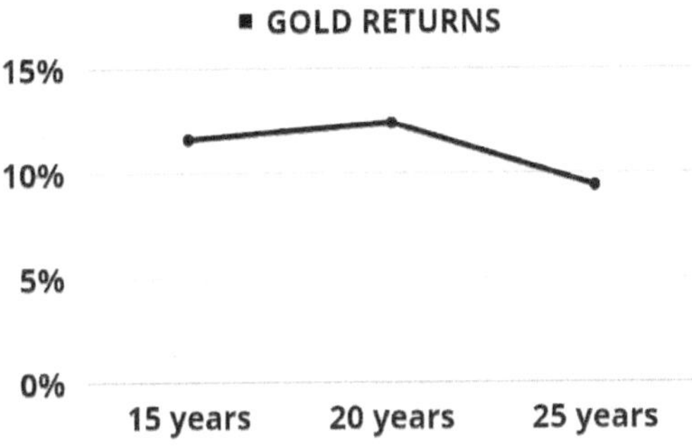

This means, at 20 years, gold itself makes 12.4% returns

Where invest 500 per month[on year -6000 rupees]

at 20 years – 12.4%

he invested 1,20,000 in gold and the estimated return is 4,07,505 rupees,

This is how money management skills are worked

I bet you!

This laborer with high money management skills can beat the doctor who earns lakhs with poor money management skills

FQ = 1,20,000

12,000 investment + 6000 on gold

at 12 % CAGR

In the long term,

His FQ boosted more than we imagine

At 20 years, the returns of the index fund and gold itself make

7,59,148 + 4,07,505 = 11,66,653 rupees

that's his 10-year salary, so he saves 10 years of his life when he lives the same pattern of money management

This why many smart peoples live a financially freedom life and some highly advanced traditional education people still praise god for salary hikes and scolded god for his poor destiny

It was most stupid nature, I see in most middle-class life

God is not responsible for our lives
Is what we do in our precious time
that reflected the destiny we are
-CG

<u>WHY ONLY 27%</u>

<u>Again you can see the graph,</u>

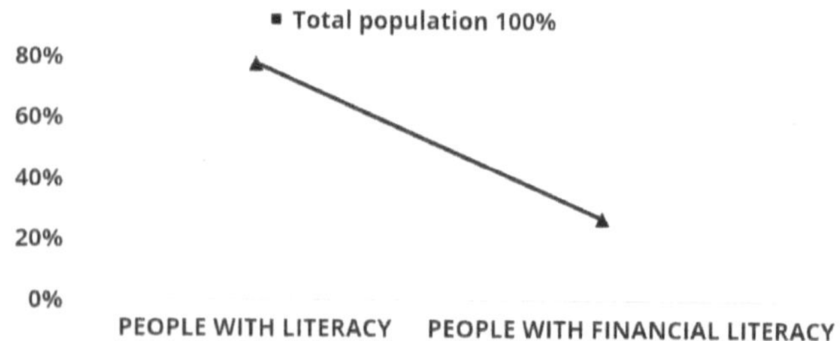

Only 27 % of the population, where well know about financial education.

But what happened to remain 73% of the population?

Traditional education: financial education ratio is

77% : 27 %

Ok! At the literacy rate, we have 77% - 27%[financial literate]

= 50 %

What happened to the 50% of literacy people? why they can't shine in financial literacy also?

I bet you, this 50% of the population is working in a job, waiting for paycheck hikes, and creating emotion with god for their destiny.

It was a disaster

The reason for the 50% population, who can't learn about financial literacy due to their traditional education systems

Even today, we see the same syllabus of 1990, which was still followed by school systems and they de-evolve the entire human ecosystem. I'm not a big fan of traditional education, where in the initial stages, it was good but people who want to do something, want to develop something extra, which was not available in school systems

When I ask my friend, did you like this subject? Many of them replied, I NEED MARKS, SO I MEMORIZE but heart truth I didn't like this.

My friend's replies devasted me because they are de-evolve, they memorize the core concept and give his protective time on MARKS!

They shine by marks by memorizing, but reality speaks something different.

So,50% population are like my friends working for marks and creating their destiny in the sand storm.

This type of learning often causes them to degrade themselves.

Again, I ask my friend about financial education, and they tell, I'm busy in my college days, so don't ask this question

When I give him a book about financial education, their replies are similar, This book was big, and IT WAS HARD TO MEMORIZE!

My heart is blocked by these answers!

SCHOOL CAN'T CHANGE BUT WE

Even schools can't change but we can,

It only develops when we change the mindset, but yeah! It was a habit, hard to break,

With proactive people as a friend, you easily beat the resistance and enjoy the reward

Today social media is a huge network for people who are searching to be proactive.

I think the 50% can't change their mindset but it changes only through education.

MY SUGGESTION

Traditional education was learned throughout childhood to teen, so my suggestion is to implement financial chapters even in 2 and 3-grade students that help to see, how the world literally works

I hear the news lot of CBSE schools, and attach a financial management paper to their curriculum, it was wonderful

Yeah! Little impact on little life that makes heaven in a hand.

HABIT OF INVESTING

It was the only habit that makes you financially free and lives a heaven life that you desire

We already see inflation is a big villain for people who save money, so they need to invest their money that makes a return for exceeds inflation

According to NATIONAL STOCK EXCHANGE[NSE],

There are 1.2 core active investors in India, a country of 138 core people, it was only 0.86%

But in recent year survey says,

They covered 47,000 households from across 39 districts, where they showed,40% of likely to invest in equity and mutual funds and 15% are investing in property, cars, and jewelry

When LIFE INSURANCE CORPORATION[LIC], offer their shares at a discount value for their policyholders that make a climbing number of Demat accounts in india[nearly 34 lakh new Demat account open for LIC IPO]

[TECHNICAL TERM

DEMAT ACCOUNT – A Account that holds financial security like a share, or bond that is traded on the share market in a digital form]

This condition was pretty well today, but we need more!

QUESTIONS YOU MAY ASK IN THIS SECTION

[1] INVESTING MAKES ME RICH?

[2] DO WE SEE RICH PEOPLE TODAY, ARE THEY INVEST THEIR MONEY IN THE SHARE MARKET?

[3] WHAT TYPE OF INVESTMENTS BILLIONAIRES MADE?

[4] WHAT TYPE OF INVESTMENT MODERN DAY LOOKS FOR?

Let's see every answer in a detailed manner

[1] INVESTING MAKES ME RICH

It was a wonderful question to answer, INVESTING IS A ONLY OPTION TO MULTIPLY YOUR MONEY, EVEN AT YOU SLEEP AT 24 HOURS A DAY

If you are a middle-class man, who wants to make core-level money in long-term thinking

there are many financial products available in the markets

Like

► INDEX FUNDS

► NIFTY BEES

► DEBT FUNDS

► HYBRID FUNDS

► INFLATION-ADJUSTED BONDS ARE ALSO AVAILABLE

These are the investment options that make a lower middle-class to middle-class level but when you invest at 50 or 75 years, I bet you will be a multimillionaire!!!!!

But I show shocking facts

As per the SEBI survey,

95% of Indian families invest their money in FD[FIXED DEPOSIT] less than 10% only invest in mutual funds!!

WARREN BUFFET ADVICE

Index funds are common in many investment options, even in May 2022, he recommend S&P 500 index fund for most people, the best thing they do.

If you break the words of Mr. warren buffet, you pay the penalty!

Just see the difference between investing in FD VS INDEX FUNDS

Let's see the interest rate of Fixed deposits in a bank

FIXED DEPOSIT INTEREST RATE[BELOW 2 CORES]	
NAME OF THE BANK	% OF INTEREST
STATE BANK OF INDIA	2.90 TO 5.50%
AXIS BANK	2.50 TO 5.75%
RBL BANK	3.25 TO 6.65%
HDFC BANK	2.50 TO 5.75%
CANARA BANK	2.90 TO 5.75%
KOTAK MAHINDRA	2.50 TO 5.90%
IDBI BANK	2.70 TO 5.60%

These interest rates are changed for senior citizens

But I didn't want to make this book for senior citizens

I want young aspirants to know the details of financial investing

So, let's take a maximum interest of 6%

Index fund[NIFTY] average return is 12%

Imagine investing 1000 per month on both FD and INDEX FUND

the difference I show in a table

Investing in FD VS Investing in INDEX FUNDS	
AT 20 YEAR PERIOD	
FIXED DEPOSIT	**INDEX FUNDS**
1 year – 12,397	1 year – 12,809
5 year – 70,119	5 year – 82,486
10 year – 1,64,699	10 year – 2,32,339
15 year – 2,92,273	15 year – 5,04,576
18 year – 3,89,290	18 year – 7,65,439
20 year – 4,64,351	20 year – 9,99,148

Just see the comparison, your heart gets storming

You see in this table, where at 5 year

FD – 70,119

IF – 82,486

The difference is only 12,367 rupees

But in 20 year

FD – 4,64,351

IF – 9,99,148

The difference is 5,34,797

In middle-class families it was considered a huge amount, so waste yours on a low investment option instead of a high one!

WHY DO PEOPLE NOT INVEST IN INDEX FUNDS

Because of a lack of knowledge or fear about share market investments

Even though of modern evolution, I ask my friend about index fund

His reply is SHARE MARKET ARE RISKY

Often most middle-class families fall into this trap

One of my favorite quotes from MARK ZUCKERBERG can change your perceptive

'The biggest risk is not taking any risk

In a world that changing really quickly,

The only strategy that is guaranteed

To fail is not to take risks

Middle-class life is not changed when you develop the skill of risk-taking!

When you understand this concept, you save 5 lakh rupees from FD to IF[INDEX FUNDS]

So, the final answer to the question is INVESTING MAKES YOU RICH, yeah! It makes but proper investing knowledge leads the destiny

WHY MIDDLE CLASS CAN'T GET SUFFICIENT INFORMATION

Because of their inner circle

You know a quote called

Birds flock together

This was the reality, that every middle class faced

Their inner circles narrow their vision which affects their wide-lens views, so they are trapped in the storm of disaster.

When you want to do something in your life, you should change your circle

As a famous saying,

'If you are in your 20's and your main circle is not discussed stocks, investments, business, then it's time to FIND A NEW CIRCLE'

GO AHEAD!

[2] DO WE SEE RICH PEOPLE TODAY, ARE THEY INVEST THEIR MONEY IN THE SHARE MARKET?

This is difficult to answer because you see today rich people are not a guy to invest in the share market but they sell their equity via shares to the public to become the wealthy persons

This was the hidden truth, only a few people learned.

HOW THEY SELL THE EQUITY VIA SHARES

Often many rich people create a profitable business, they need to develop their company to the next level or they prefer to sell the ownership stake of their company, to withdraw their equity and something they desire

So, they go to the share market and sell their stake via shares to the public

They bid the price of the share based on the requirements of the company's future prospects

For example – ABC LTD owner sell his stake in his company, he bet 200 per share, where he sold 5 % of his stake, let's imagine 5 % means 10 lakh share

If he sells,

200 * 10 lakh share

= 2000 lakh rupees [20 cores rupees]

He makes it by simply selling his 5 % stake, imagine a middle-class job man making 20 cores, even an index fund takes 40+ years to make it!

This was the POWER OF BUSINESS

It was the method, where rich was used!

Many people misunderstand business people as profiting only from sales of the business

But it's not

They profit in a lot of ways

Even you see a lot of billionaires today have a public limited company, where it trades on the share market

So, their equity goes up and down due to market oscillation

Example – Elon musk[tesla],jeff bezos[amazon],bill gates[microsoft],mark zuckerberg[meta]

In India,Ratan tata[tata steel,motors,consulting service]mukesh ambani[reliance],Gautam adani[adani ports etc],Sunil mittal[aritel],R.K Damani [d mart]

These are the leading businessman whose net worth is billions by selling their equity in the share market.

Even everyone knows Falguni Nayar, Founder of NYAKA, before his company went public, she and her family's stake was worth 27,962 cores but when his company go public, the valuation of his company skyrocketed and Nayar and her family's net worth hits 54,831 core rupees.

The ipo[initial public offering] helps her to place his name on INDIA'S RICHEST SELF-MADE WOMEN BILLIONAIRE LIST.

[TECHNICAL TERM

IPO – INITIAL PUBLIC OFFERING

it was an offer for the public created by an owner of the company, to raise the fund via public or sell his stake via public

When a company needs funds to level up its growth, they have many options to raise, it may go to VENTURE CAPITALIST OR ANGEL INVESTORS ETC but if they need the public to get his offer to raise their money, they go IPO with help of SEBI, on this stage they raise their money by issuing shares or if the company owner wants to sell his stake, he foremost determines, which part of equity is diluted, if the ownership interest to sell his 5% stake, he must value this based on company market value then he determines the price of a share and they sell it via public.

Let's see the difference between

<u>*SELLING A SHARE VS INVESTING A SHARE*</u>

SELLING A SHARE VS INVESTING A SHARE

SELLING A SHARE	INVESTING A SHARE
You need business to sell your share	You doesn't need business to invest
Control of your business is done buy[when you have a major shareholding]	When investor contain major stake,he controls the company but they not involve in active manner
You easily make profits by issuing IPO	They make profits only through compounding by his best investments compare to selling a share,investing a share make small profits
It helps to achieve a level of richness in quick manner,once you have a profitable business	It takes time to build
Once you sell your company share,via public,your company valuation and brand power hits pikes	Investing a company not make you fame but it create a fame when you have huge stake on the company[when you have a huge stake,you considered as a owners,so the difference is change based on your stake]
Many business owners have a dream to build a business and create their valuation in huge and	Often majority of investment come from mutual funds,it was only considered as a purpose of pension
sell their hole stake in public that helps them to hit a financial freedom level at young years and they do it again and again to become millionaires	or other long term money making option but compare with selling,it was a slow lane process
Some other points are	
You have power of your internal management balance sheet	They have only power on external balance sheet
Owners have a power to manipulate company profit by doing window dressing related activities,that helps to calm down the investors [but it was not recommend]	They don't known the internal activity,but if they find any fault on company activities,they have a voting power to raise the question,even he had a rights to fire the employees.

SELLING VS INVESTING

Once you understand the difference between investing a share and selling a share,

I think you clean your eye lens with a gold cloth because it was the key insight that makes a business owner into a ton of cash

[CAUTION – Selling a 25% stake in public is not a big concern, because as per SEBI, the owner only owns a 75% stake, so 25% is not a dead path

But when your stake reduces by more than 90%, it creates a big problem for your brand and even causes investors tremendous stress, But if you have an interest to start a new company, You should make your old business system as effective as possible when any new one buys your company, First and foremost he checks about BUSINESS SYSTEM.

When you have a good business system, he may premium for your business, when you handle your business with an effective system, it also saves investors money and their confidence

In simple words – while selling your whole stake, you must make a good business system,

Even a high school student understands your system that makes everyone happy!]

But a lot of business owners often come to the share market to raise their net worth and they get to develop their business without selling their stake because they believe in their company value and worth & future levels not for selling a share to become billionaires

This was the answer to the second question

Selling a share to make a value instead of investing

'Once you understand the key patterns

You break the lock without a key'.

[3] WHAT TYPE OF INVESTMENTS BILLIONAIRES MADE?

When you search this question on google, it comes to the result:

They invest in money market mutual funds, certificates of deposits, commercial papers, and treasury bills

And they also invest on

►private and commercial real estate

►land

►gold

►artworks

Often people misunderstand their investment strategies

BILLIONAIRES DO NOT INVEST IN RICHES

It was the hidden truth, but often middle class didn't know.

Many things investing in money markets, and mutual funds make him rich in a short time but it takes huge

Billionaires invest their money to prevent inflation drain, but it was misunderstood by the middle class, to invest this and make a billion

They become rich by building a business or powerful network that helps them to earn billions, by protecting their money from inflation and economic drainage situation, they invest it in low-risk investments and gold-like metals

When the middle class invests their money in what google shows like

MONEY MARKET MUTUAL FUNDS

CERTIFICATE OF DEPOSITS

TREASURY BILLS

Let's take an example – where they aim for 20 years to become rich

Consider inflation as a factor also

MONEY MARKET

First, what is the money market?

A market for debt securities, who seek to borrow and lend money on a short-term period

Let's see the best money market mutual funds returns in India at a 1 to 10-year period

BEST MONEY MARKET MUTUAL FUNDS IN INDIA				
MUTUAL FUND SCHEME	1 YEAR [RETURN]	3 YEAR	5 YEAR	10 YEAR
L&T MONEY MARKET FUND	8%	7.6%	8.1 %	8.3 %
ADITIYA BIRLA SUN LIFE MONEY MANAGER FUND	7.9%	7.6%	7.7%	8.2%
FRANKLIN INDIA SAVINGS FUND	8.2 %	7.6%	7.8%	8.2%
KOTAK MONEY MARKET FUNDS	7.7%	7.4%	7.6%	8.1%
NIPPON INDIA MONEY MARKET FUND	7.8%	7.5%	7.6%	8.1%

Money market mutual funds are less risky than normal mutual funds[invest on share market]

So, they give fewer returns than normal mutual funds

let's take 8.3% interest on 10 years by L&T money market fund

I invest 1000 rupees in it,

The result :

My investment amount is 1,20,000

Estimate returns – 67,327[8.3% compounding every year]

The total value is 1,87,327

It was a slow lane process,

You see today billionaires are made by this investment

The answer is NO !!!!!!!!!!!!!!!!!!!!!!!!!!!!!!!!!!

They can't become rich with this investment, they only invest for inflation protection

So, please understand the difference between investing to the rich and just adjusted investment for inflation

I show you another shocking fact

MUTUAL FUNDS				
INCOME SLAB	NUMBER OF UNIQUE INVESTORS	% OF TOTAL INDIVIDUAL INVESTORS	AUM[IN Cr]	% AUM
Less than Rs.1 lakh	16,33,909	8.80%	1,44,363.71	4.50%
Rs.1 – Rs 5 lakh	1,13,66,741	61.21%	7,71,650.59	24.04%
Rs 5 -Rs 10 lakh	35,81,287	19.28%	5,98,459.05	18.64%
Rs 10 – Rs 25 lakh	14,31,613	7.71%	3,61,744.41	11.27%
Rs 25 – Rs 1 core	4,22,131	2.27%	3,40,640	10.61%
Rs 1 -5 core	1,35,446	0.73%	9,93,121.66	30.93%
More than 5 core	245	0.00%	408.86	0.01%

See this table, you can see Rs 1 -5 lakh people who dominate in mutual funds, this type of people are middle class

They looking for their investment to become rich

You see, where increasing incomes show a decrease in unique investors

More than 5 core categories have only 245 unique investors, this is why I tell, rich people are not looking for investment to rich, they are rich by their business or but in this slab often it was high executive employees, who also make huge money on their paychecks, looking for the mutual fund as a tool for asset construction, and not for the richness

So,

Points to remember are

Rich people don't invest in the mutual fund for richness, they invest only for protection due to inflation or some little asset creation

Let's see other investments

CERTIFICATE OF DEPOSIT AND TREASURY BILLS

They are a risk-free investment and give a guaranteed return[but low interest]

It only used to balance our money to inflation

List of banks that provide certificates of deposits

CERTIFICATE OF DEPOSITS	
BANKS	AVERAGE YIELD PER YEAR
Axis bank	7 %
Hdfc bank	7.07%
Icici bank	6.93 %
Yes bank	7.19%
Idfc bank	6.84%

Bank of baroda	6.70%
Rbl bank	7.03%

The average interest rate for a certificate of deposit is [just take 7%], why do rich peoples invest this?

As the same as protection from inflation

India inflation rate = just take[7%]

So, the rich people invest in this scheme, it eventually protects their money from inflation

India inflation = certificate of deposit[interest rate]

7% = 7%

So, it will balance, and the rich can't lose the purchasing power of their money

TREASURY BILLS

What are treasury bills?

It was the short-term debt instrument issued by the government of India, to raise funds from the public and repayment at later date with interest

It was three types
[1] 91-day bill
[2] 182-day bill
[3] 364-day bill

TREASURY BILLS INTEREST RATE YIELD	
DAY BILLS	% INTEREST [JUL 2022 DATA]
91 DAY BILLS	5.40%
182 DAY BILLS	5.85%
364 DAY BILLS	6.24 %

As per inflation data,
Treasury bills can't beat down inflation based on their interest rate
when you invest in 364-day bills,
The interest rate is 6.24%
But inflation is 7%
it can balance when inflation is lower than 7%
But yeah! Again they only invest in Inflation adjustments
and finally commercial papers
It is also a debt instrument issued by corporate companies, for short-term debt obligation, commonly it was issued by good credit-rating companies
It also has an interest rate of 3.82 – 4.08%
So, it is also used for inflation adjustments.

THE GOOGLE ANSWER IS WRONG

NO! It depends on your question
[3] question is

WHAT TYPE OF INVESTMENTS BILLIONAIRES MADE?

So, the question is

What type of investment where BILLIONAIRE made

Highlight the word, BILLIONAIRE

Which means you ask a question about

Where billionaire[the man who become rich & not looking for rich] their investment

In simple words, which investments rich people made?

But most middle classes misunderstand this question

They think this investment made him rich but it was not ...

so, please understand

Google's answer is not wrong, but your understanding........

And we see other investment categories

[1] PRIVATE AND COMMERCIAL REAL ESTATE

[2] LAND

[3] GOLD

[4] ARTWORK

According to the reserve bank of India,

Tracking house prices in 10 major cities of India by India's house price index

It shows the data of the last 10 years, the real estate sector compounded at 11.6% per year

In the last 10 years,

Commercial properties compounded at 9.5%

Residential properties compounded at 9.5%

REIT[Real estate investment trust] at 11.8%

REAL ESTATE RETURNS IN INDIA

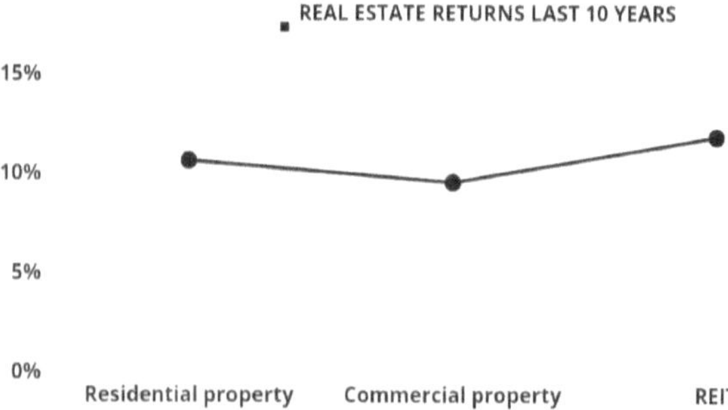

Often real estate investments are so costly, they can't be afforded by middle-class families

So, only the new investment option is REIT[Real estate investment trust]

In this model, they involve buying real estate, leasing space, or financing commercial properties, etc by the investment collected by the public.

They give 90% of their returns to investors via dividends

It was a wonderful option for people who looking for passive income but did not have much money to build a house

It was a good investment option for rich people to grow their money in 5 to 10 periods

It was good for the middle class also but it can't make you rich like a billionaire, it makes but it takes compounding[that takes more than 50 years]

If you are in 20 years, it takes 50+ years to become rich level,

I think it was a slow lane process

EVERGREEN INVESTMENTS

Land and gold were the primary advice for every middle-class family

It was a good investment for people in the middle class, but yeah! Again, this leads to years !!!!!!!!!

ARTWORK

Rich people invest in artwork for two reasons

[1] because they like artwork

[2] when the artwork was demanded, they invest their money because this make them pride[because of demand]

Artwork like MONA LISA is worth believed more than $850 million dollars and on May 14, 2015, PICASSO -WOMEN OF ALGIERS' version painting sold out on auction at $179,365,000.

Due to rare and demand, many billionaires invest in artworks

Artwork is commonly a risky investment because it often goes in and out of style that leads to affect the resale value

But they didn't feel it was an investment, they considered only the ancientness and skills of the artist.

I discuss artwork in the next question on the modern way.

[4] WHAT TYPE OF INVESTMENT DOES THE MODERN DAY LOOK FOR?

Today in this modern days

Investment like

►CRYPTO

►METAVERSE

►NFT

are most popular

But India poses 30 % +[surcharge and cess] to crypto investments

I think blockchain is the leading revolution we can see in the modern days

When I get started to study crypto investing, I literally shocked, I just tell my mind, how the world will change in 10 -20 years!!!!!!!!!!

I didn't recommend investing in crypto, because it was traded 24*7, so it was a high-risk and high-reward game.

Some famous cryptos are

[1] ETHEREUM [ETH]

[2] BITCOIN [BTC]

[3] RIPPLE [XRP]

[4] APECOIN [APE]

[5] BINANCE COIN [BNB]

I am not an expert in crypto, but it was an investment option available in modern days

So early learning leads to early earns

[2] METAVERSE

When Mark Zuckerberg announce by META, My metaverse studies leads to happen

I think the FUTURE IS FASTER THAN I THINK

This wide approach lead my thinking into some special world!

When they tell about investment in VIRTUAL LAND on metaverse, I am shocked at many facial expressions!!!!

The recent news comes on DUBAI, they launched DUBAI METAVERSE, and they plan to create 40,000 jobs in the metaverse and plan to boost their GDP by $4 billion

Google also builds its own operating system for metaverse, and they invest nearly $40 million in metaverse projects

Virtual land investing in the metaverse is also so famous in modern days like real estate but it was so modern than we imagine

[3] NFT

NFT means NON FUNGIBLE TOKENS, they link ownership to the digital asset, the asset may be arts, music, video, etc

We see billionaires invest in the artwork on [3] question, same as many billionaires today have an interest in NFTS because it was limited and has unique identification codes

Many artists prefer to sell their art via NFT, which creates a unique status for the buyer

The most expensive NFT art is THE MERGE, which was sold at $91.8 million, Now you think about the scope of NFT ART?

In India, Amitabh Bachchan's NFT is considered an expensive NFT that sold for Rs.7.18 core approx

This type of investment gives prestige to rich man life, even many yacht parties were conducted through NFT as an entry pass.....

These were the modern-day investments, those rich people looking for.

IMPORTANT POINT OF THIS TOPIC

There is a huge difference between

The habit of saving vs the habit of investing

In today's world, a lot of people can't get awareness about the share market, index funds, etc

They follow the same strategies that their generation told them, where they still save the money and think it was a good investment[inflation boils everything, MIND IT!]

Habit formation often comes through what type of thinking we have in this world,

Suppose, you are in a middle-class family like me, the words of your parents and friends are getting influenced by your subconscious mind that makes a habit of limiting factors

Once you know the difference between the habit of saving and investing, you will get a gem!

So, only I explain in detail about investing because this type of knowledge often can't share by your circle of influence

It was my duty to influence you to give a correct track

We already see an example of how one invests in FD to get a rich dream vs How one invests in Index funds to have a rich dream the % of interest breaks everything, Do you ever imagine?

Often most people, don't understand this type of investment, and they tell IT WAS RISKY,

Guess what?

It was shared from generation to generation that ruins the entire life of the particular family tree.

So, understand the habit patterns that ancient people developed for us and understand the modern-day methods

According to Charles duhigg,

The habit was formed by

► CUE

► ROUTINE

► REWARD

I give you a CUE, so the routine of the habit of saving vs investing is done by you and the reward stands in your hands

But understand

My simple notes

Working in a job, looking for an index fund to get rich, it takes more than 50+ years to get the high-end life[on the time, you spend more time on your wheelchair instead of your investment returns

OR

Building a business at a young age to solve people's problems gives value to your life, once you develop a system, Yeah! You are financially free and enjoy your life at a young age when you become a rich man, it was easy to invest in an index fund to make returns and protect your money from inflation!!!!

THE CHOICE IS YOURS!

One thing can change you,

HABIT

Let me give one final example of

Investing in an index fund at 5 lakh and investing in an index fund at 1000

See the table below

where we invest 1000 on 20 year period at a 12% return

1 year - 12809
2 year – 27,243
3 year – 43,508
4 year – 61,835
5 year – 82,486
6 year – 1,05,707
7 year – 1,31,979

8 year – 1,61,527
9 year – 1,94,822
10 year -2,32,339
11 year – 2,74,615
12 year – 3,22,252
13 year – 3,75,931
14 year – 4,36,418
15 year – 5,04,576

Imagine it takes 15 years for 1000 to change 5 lakh rupees

If I ask a question,

where you invest 5 lakh instead of 1000, I can save 15 years of 1000 rupees compounding,

Let me explain in detail, in the table

1000 rupee per month guy	5 lakh per month guy
15 year – 5,04,576	1 year – 64,04,664
16 year – 5,81,378	
17 year – 6,67,921	
18 year – 7,65,439	
19 year – 8,75,325	
20 year – 9,99,148	
21 year – 11,38,674	
22 year – 12,95,896	
23 year – 14,73,057	
24 year – 16,72,689	
25 year – 18,97,635	

Imagine 25 year period[1000 turns into 18 lakh rupee] but we see 5 lakh per month guy[1 year = 64 lakhs]

That's it!

This why investing in the rich makes you multiply your money at huge than a small penny!!!

Let's see the table of 25 years, how this 5lakh guy's money compounded

1 year – 64,04,664
2 year – 1,36,21,600
3 year – 2,17,53,824
4 year – 3,09,17,417
5 year – 4,12,43,183
6 year – 5,28,78,515
7 year – 6,59,89,499
8 year – 8,07,63,283
9 year – 9,74,10,753
10 year – 11,61,69,538
11 year – 13,73,07,407
12 year – 16,11,26,087
13 year -18,79,65,572
14 year – 21,82,08,976
15 year – 25,22,88,000
16 year – 29,06,89,097
17 year – 33,39,60,414
18 year -38,27,19,618
19 year – 43,76,62,709
20 year – 49,95,73,960
21 year – 56,93,37,106
22 year – 64,79,47,966
23 year – 73,65,28,650
24 year – 83,63,43,582

25 year – 94,88,17,546
26 year – 107,55,56,024

5 lakh into 100 cores

In **26 year** period, your **5 lakh per month** investment turns into **100 core rupee**

Whereas some 1000 per month guy returns are devastating compared with 5 lakh guy

In a simple graph of these two examples,

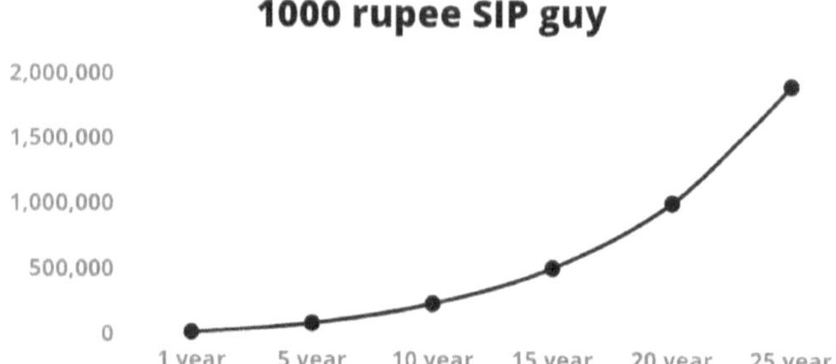

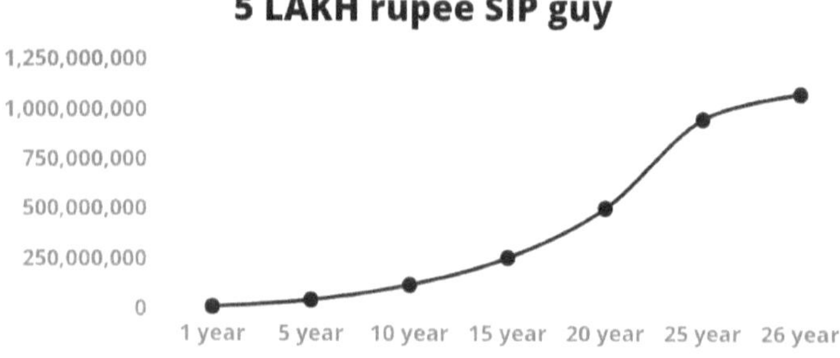

This way I tell, the rich to use index funds for asset building and not to become rich

Middle class working a job and investing index funds and think, one day I'm in ROLLS ROYCE

IT WAS FOOLISHNESS!!!!

So, this was the game totally done by

How your habit replicates.......

Your life is determined by your habits

A small percentage of difference in interest can make you or breaks you!

A small change in your habits

leads to a change in the whole destiny you imagine!

CHAPTER THIRTEEN

LAW OF ATTRACTION

One of the most interesting topics, that change my destiny into a new phase

HOW THE LAW OF ATTRACTION WORKS IN MY LIFE

In my 15-16 years, I have had a habit to get influenced by motivational videos, I get a firestorm in my eyes, and tell my spirit

WE WANT TO DO SOMETHING SPECIAL!

These lines create a big impact on my life.

Once I understand the concept of believing in the law of attraction, my life starts to get change !!

A DREAM OF ROLLS ROYCE

When my friend introduced me to Rolls Royce, I get shocked by the facts Rolls Royce has.

I bet my friend! One day I will buy one ROLLS ROYCE!

He smiles and tells me, you can't AFFORD THAT.

These words hit my threshold level, and tell my friend, it was not afforded by you but not mine!

And then the conversation leaves,

My friend thinks, I just say the words to finish the conversation.

But I was so fired on this topic, my spirit starts to burn the way, First time MY SPIRIT SPEAKS TO ME

LET'S MOVE CG!

CREATE OUR DESTINY WITH OUR OWN HANDS!!!!!

I didn't know how to buy a Rolls Royce

Where only one I have is MY BELIEF

I eat with Rolls Royce thoughts, I drink water with Rolls Royce thoughts, I Imagine the ROLLS ROYCE ENTRY, what I will do in future

I sleep with Rolls Royce dreams,

One day, a funny matter also happened, On one night, I just sleep a regular manner, and suddenly I woke up and shouted ROLLS ROYCE, where my brother near me, thinks I WAS INSANE

So, this type of impact, that Rolls Royce create on my life,

But again I didn't know, how to buy Rolls Royce

This belief makes me do something special, like reading a book, or listening billionaire's activities on youtube, that make a huge impact on my life

Small changes in my activity lead to creating different thinking, which I have never seen before.

This belief create my book reading habits and financial management skills that make me think, ROLLS ROYCE WAS A EASY TASK, IS ABOUT WHAT YOU DO ON YOUR PRECIOUS TIME!

ENTRY OF SECRET

While reading a lot of books, I get a book name called 'THE SECRET – BY RHONDA BYRNE'

This book discusses the LAW OF ATTRACTION, but the surprise is I ALREADY FOLLOW the LAW OF ATTRACTION, but I didn't know this was the law of attraction

After reading the Secret book, Yeah! My belief system level boost up, Again my favorite ' I see the world with different lens'

On the occasion of this event, I have fallen in love with KERALA, because of the nature and the culture of Kerala

I also feel my emotion and their mix with my belief system,

Guess what?

Whenever I go to college, I see nearly 4-7 Kerala vehicles on my route, which creates goosebumps for me!

And my mind floated on a Kerala dream, and my mouth makes a simple simile when I look at a Kerala vehicle

But these dream thoughts get huge influenced me to remember Vehicle numbers and districts of Kerala

Whenever I see a Kerala vehicle, I just feel the LAW OF ATTRACTION IS WORKING!

This belief makes my life into a new world, and I advise my friends to get to see the secret movie on youtube or give my secret book to them.

But they tell

SECRET IS NOT WORK FOR US

then I understood their belief system.

WHY THE LAW OF ATTRACTION IS NOT WORKING

As per the secret book,

The first and foremost rule is

BELIEVE

My friends have a poor belief system that makes to think about it, it was not working, JUST GIVE UP!!

So, it did not work for them.

The not only law of attraction or anything big you want to do in your life or create a huge revolution in human evolution,this type of dreams only occur first on the BELIEF SYSTEM

When you have a poor belief, I AM SORRY

YOU ARE THE ONLY ENEMY OF YOUR GROWTH

Big or small, just believe because once you believe, YOUR LIFE STARTS TO CHANGE,

It's time to change your life!

Go ahead, buddy !!!!!!

I have a strong belief system then why the law of attraction is not working for me?

The answer is simple,

The Law of attraction on works on you but you pause it!

Let me explain

The Law of attraction attracts things that you believe,

If in my case,

I have a dream to buy a ROLLS ROYCE

Once my belief mixed with my emotions, I start to work on it, which attracted a lot of books to me and lots of webinars to me, then I understand the roles

Today I have the knowledge to get a map about how to buy a ROLLS ROYCE,

So, it works for me

Law of attraction – attract the things to you, but you think I am busy, I just postpone it, then again the opportunities come, but the same attitude plays a role

And later, you mix with your poor circle of influence that causes to damage your attraction level, then it was act like a blow of ballon.

When you again attract the dream things, opportunities come, it is about how you use them!

I use it! Today I see a difference!

This was the power of the law of attraction

Let's see the difference between a guy with the law of attraction and another without it

A GUY WITH LAW OF ATTRACTION	WITHOUT LAW OF ATTRACTION
Strong belief system on there dream	Worst belief system on there dream
Have a positive attitude in every approach	Have a negative or neutral mindset
They have a big dreams and tell there dream at bold manner	They have a dream,fear to tell others
Have a growth mindset	Have a fixed mindset
They never doubt about failures	They doubt everything they do

WITH VS WITHOUT LOA

Everything in our life comes only through the
BELIEF SYSTEM WE HAVE

I also hear a lot of quires from my friends and they ask me a simple question

WHAT ARE THE STEPS I NEED TO DO

TO GET THE LAW OF ATTRACTION WORK IN MY LIFE?

It was a good question,

where my readers those who have this problem, don't worry

Just follow some simple steps, and you will get the gem

[1] STAY IN A POSITIVE MOOD AND REDUCE YOUR NEGATIVITY

[2] MAKE A BOND WITH A POSITIVE ATTITUDE TOWARD PEOPLE

[3] REDUCE DOUBT ON YOUR PATH

[4] BELIEF + WORKS = SUCCESS

[5] ALWAYS HAVE A COURAGEOUS BELIEF, WHENEVER ANYTHING CROSSES ON YOUR PATH[MAY BE FAILURES OR ANY]

We just read the steps and move on

But it can't make an impact until

Your belief system mixes with emotions that lead to success but only occur, once you start working!

Every successful people today, have a positive attitude with a good work ethic,

The work ethic leads to search a lot of new things

That leads to mind evolution

when it starts, your journey to build your dream life is like a hand of a small distance !!

ANCIENT BELIEF OF THE LAW OF ATTRACTION

When I get insights about the law of attraction, I just see the belief where I get in god

Through this universe, whenever I pray for god, I didn't tell my desires to god, which means I tell my desire to mine[my subconscious mind]

When my subconscious mind converts my desire into a belief system, where it mixes with my emotion, Yeah! LAW OF ATTRACTION starts to work !!!

This belief was developed by ancients, but through civilization and many social cultures, it will act on but through a different form

Put into the simple words

DIFFERENT RELIGIONS ARE DIFFERENT DOORS OF THE SAME HOUSE

The house was our BELIEF SYSTEM

MY BELIEF SYSTEM

When my mom told me, to pray the god, where she approached me to go to the temple or do culturally related things

In the initial stage of my life, I have the good grace of god, whenever I fall into a trap, or hot desire to achieve, I suddenly start praying

GOD ! PLEASE HELP ME!

I NEED THIS!

PLEASE BUY IT FOR ME !!!

PLEASE !!!!!!

With a tear in my eyes, I just pray about my childhood years

But once I understand the concept of the LAW OF ATTRACTION

Then I realized, I'm not praying to god, I just pray with my subconscious mind that derives my belief system, and my tears of praying led my emotion part to active, then the belief and emotion mix, where the law of attraction starts to work on

In simple words,

BELIEF + EMOTION = LAW OF ATTRACTION
This leads my understanding to the next level

PAIN IN MY BODY

Whenever I feel pain in my body or any ailments,i just pray to god,
like,
GOD PLEASE SAVE ME!
I AM A SMALL GUY,
I CAN'T HAVE THE POWER TO FEEL THE PAIN
SO, PLEASE CURE IT !!!!
with tears in my eyes........
When I understand, LAW OF ATTRACTION,
Yeah! I just pray to my subconscious, to cure this disease and they cure it!
But I think it was done by god, through the real answer is
YOUR POWER OF SUBCONSCIOUS MIND
Then I understand my subconscious power, and I get a gem
Most diseases have not come to our bodies, it's only come through our mind
Once you make your mind so proactive or productive, where your body starts to cure!!!!
I implement this law into my life, when I am in heavy fever, my mom recommends me medicine, But I did not like it because of bitterness!
So, I just pray to my subconscious, to cure this disease with emotional words.
After some days, I easily recover from this disease in a happy mood and without medicine
Because of my power of subconscious !!

HOW DREAMS ACHIEVED BY THE LAW OF ATTRACTION WITH THE HELP OF SUBCONSCIOUS

Even though I have dreamed about achieving some things, first and foremost I pray to my subconscious and make an image of my success party and I speak to my SPIRIT, what we do to achieve this target?

My spirit tells you to want to do this. Do you want to do that?

I can't hesitate about any movement, I just follow my spirit words, and believe it will happen, that's it!

I get succeed

Let me give a live example of my life

TRIGONOMETRY SUCCESS

On my 10 standards, there was a maths teacher, I can't mention his name but he was a workaholic in his character, he conducted a maths exam, I tell my dad about this exam.

At the time, I have a dream about the mobile tabs. Where my dad told me, once you get a 90+ mark in your maths exam, I can buy one tab for you !!!

I was so excited, and think about tab every night!!

It was registered in my subconscious mind, the calling of my spirit also comes in but I hesitate and I didn't do any work for the exam, I just have dreams every day

When the exam was conducted, I wrote it, then the result came

Guess what?

I only take 70 marks out of 100 instead of 90+ marks, in my class, everyone I see gets 90+ marks, and my best friends get 95+ marks....

I cried in my school, and my spirits get the threshold level, where the heat in my head starts to build on

And I go to my home, my father asked me the result, I told, noting bad only 70 marks, My dad scolded me and tell,

YOU ARE BETTER,

Let's take this mark on another test,

He asks me, what is the next test,

I replied trigonometry, His belief was crushed, because it was the hardest subject in maths

My dad move on!

No belief !! I cried a lot !!!!

Then after some time, My spirit start to speak with me about this failure

CG! I TOLD YOU TO DO THE WORK

BUT YOU HESITATE

OK! COOL RELAX! LIFE IS LONG

PREPARE FOR THE NEXT EXAM!

But I told my spirit, it was trigonometry,

very very hard subject !!

My spirits tell, OK! IT'S NOT A HARD SUBJECT LIKE ROCKET

THIS WAS THE EASIEST SUBJECT YOU EVER SEE

BECAUSE IT ALSO CREATED BY A HUMANS

IT'S NOT CREATED BY ALIENS

UNDERSTAND IT! PLEASE!

STUDY CG! I WILL HELP YOU

These words of my spirit guide me, to get study trigonometry

In this part,

I have a belief system +

emotions +

subconscious grace +

law of attraction roles+

work ethic = success

Yeah! I succeed, I get 96 marks on trigonometry, whereas my friends get only 50+ marks, I make it!

This happiness makes my day,

Then I understand the whole concept of a belief system for success

For achieving a new one or to get your dream into reality, you just know this formula efficiently

BELIEF SYSTEM + EMOTIONS + SUBCONSCIOUS GRACE + LAW OF ATTRACTION ROLE + WORK ETHIC = SUCCESS

Once you understand this, I bet you

You are more unique than the rest of the world....

In next chapter we see about how 1% people live their life and how they outsmart everyone...

Let' see..........................

CHAPTER FOURTEEN

1% CLUB

1 % Club is also known as an extraordinary club, where people who have a revolutionary idea have a membership in this club

WHAT ARE THE RULES IN THE 1% CLUB?

The name that tells an answer, this club is only for 1%, which means out of 100 % percent population, this club created only for 1% of the people

Which people are considered as 1%?

►The people who have a dream to create value in their life

►People with wide thinking

►people with humanity

►Mostly people with a strong work ethic

►Powerful desires, In Napolean hill's terms[BURNING DESIRE]

►People who don't get depressed by other people's activity

►People who love actions instead of words

►People who have a growth mindset

and many & many points, we can write.....

Difference between ordinary vs extraordinary

ORDINARY PEOPLE	EXTRAORDINARY PEOPLE
People who didn't have a value in there life	They have a strong value in there life,in victor franklin terms,PURPOSE
They think,i am a intelligent,and they can't touch a book by there hands	They also think, I am a intelligent,and they books on there hands for constant evolution
They trade there time for money	They trade there time for skill upgrading
They have poor work ethic	They have strong work ethic
THEY FOLLOW GIRLS	**THEY FOLLOW BOOKS**
THEY FOLLOW ACTRESS	THEY FOLLOW MENTORS
They have a spenting habit	They have a investing habit
There are narrow thinkers	They are critical or wide thinkers
They spread goosip about others	They helps others to solve there problems

ORDINARY VS EXTRAORDINARY

This was the huge difference between an ordinary and an extraordinary man or a 99% vs 1% difference

HOW TO BE A 1%

This was a big question for me to get an answer to because I am also in WORK IN PROGRESS MODE

But through my master's teaching and my books teaching, I get a point, to how to be a 1%

When I think about 1%

My mind suddenly tells me a name called ELON MUSK

Yeah! He is my inspiration

Once you understand his work ethic, you easily get a 1% club seat.

When I study his life rules and his thinking patterns, I get a reservation of 1%

ELON MUSK TOP LIFE RULE

[1] SEE THINGS FROM A BASIC LEVEL

[2] NEVER GIVE UP ATTITUDE

[3] COURAGE TO TAKE A RISK

[4] WORK SUPER HARD

[5] DRIVE INNOVATION

[6] EXPECTED TO FAIL

[7] ATTRACT GREAT PEOPLE

[8] DO SOMETHING IMPORTANT EVEN ODDS ARE NOT IN YOUR FAVOR

[9] BE A ADVENTURER

[10] BELIEVE IN YOURSELF, IGNORE THE NAYSAYERS

FIRST LEVEL THINKING

You see them, 1st rule - SEE THINGS FROM BASIC LEVEL

It was the only rule when you develop a new skill when you have a strong basement that gives you the confidence to build a skyscraper!

First-level thinking was the skill, I learn from Elon musk

Ok! What is first-level thinking?

This was the thinking that evolve from base to advance.

For example – You have a dinner with your loved ones[imagine], where you cut a piece of apple, and give it to your loved ones, while eating, your loved one face has to change, because of the taste of the apple[little sour +

sweet]

On time what do you think?

Apple has some diseases, so only It affects the taste of the apple, the problem is only with the apple!

It was the answer for most people!

When it comes to first-level thinking, it was different

The problem with apple does not come from automatic, they come from the apple tree, while analyzing the apple tree, we get the point, once you understand the apple tree, where you see all apple have the same taste with the same disease, so the problem is not an apple, is apple tree but how apple tree is affected?

By analyzing their roots, we can get the point, but through continuous analyzing you get a point root was not a problem, soil was!

When the soil has poor minerals, it absorbs by a root, which reduces apple immune strength, makes the apple tree to weak, and causes diseases, that cause to affect the taste of the apples

The real answer is low soil minerals, not apples!!!!!

This was the power of first-level thinking

By understanding the basics of the tree, you understand the whole system of the tree.

This help to see the accurate data of the problems.

MINDSET OF 1%

It was the most unique topic to discuss because mindset was the only tool that develop very successful people in the marketplace. They have a strong work ethic and a burning desire to lead their life and their destiny to the top level.

They don't hear what others peoples say about them and speak only on actions, not words, they have an innovative mindset, to see the opportunities or the problems that people face in daily life

They sacrifice everything for their dreams because they can't come to the world for a living, they come to create value for human evolution, and place their name in history books!!

1% of club people only have a few friends, but the few have the power to create an ocean, they believe in their friends as much as he.

They even sacrifice their sleep for their dream, BECAUSE WE HAVE ONLY 24 HOURS IN 1DAY

So, they have not spent much time on sleep, they have value in their life to sacrifice their sleep and they wake up in the morning.

In simple terms, THE 1% MINDSET IS LIVE WITH A PURPOSE

WHY 99% OF PEOPLE FAIL IN THEIR LIFE

The reason is so simple because of their HABITS

we can separate this 99% into four parts

[1] 30 %

[2] 50%

[3] 10%

[4] 9%

[1] 30% of peoples

They are poor people who have

▶ POOR HABITS

►POOR CIRCUMSTANCES

►POOR CIRCLE OF INFLUENCE

►POOR THINKING

and on and on.......

We can't change these people's lives because it was a hard task, and even can't understand what we are speaking to them.

They simply manipulate by their external circumstance and live their life, but the sad story is?

The same habits and personalities that follow from generation to generation make tremendous disasters in future lives

The one thing that helps this type of people is EDUCATION

The government also provides a lot of incentives to this type of people, but it was misused by their families, Children in this 30% have spending habits than an investing habit

This makes them out of balance immediately, this ways force them to work instead of education

Ok! I can't write this topic too long, because yeah !............

[2] 50 % of people

These types of people are middle class, they have

►GRADUATE DEGREE

► MARKS-ORIENTED MINDSET

►LOOKING FOR HIGH PAYING JOB

►DREAM TO LIVE LUXURY LIFE

►PARTIES

►BIG CONSUMERS

Why India is the best for many corporates world?

Because of this 50% population guys, they are the big consumers in India

Often these guys have a graduate degree and looking for a high-paying job, or government job.

They only focus on money, not value, this makes them live a stagnant life and not a momentum one

We can change these people through EDUCATION

But you may ask, if they have a graduate degree, then why do they need education?

Most people can't understand the difference between Traditional and financial education[we discuss this topic in previous chapters] they have good ethics on traditional education but they have poor financial education

While providing financial education to these guys, I bet you they can change their mindset

Even in this stage that manipulation comes at

GOOD MARKS LEAD TO GOVERNMENT JOB

That leads our economy to shrinkage

What I mean by that is when people focus on government jobs because it was stable and the salary comes at the correct time!

Ok! I just ask one question.

If you are a business owner, you appoint a guy with a high degree, but his purpose of joining your company is a big salary, he just sits simply and does little work and asks you for a huge pay

Do you pay for it or not?

The answer you know!

The same as a government job, but in this case, the government pays you a salary, where the little work you done but makes a huge impact on the economy, through the poor service, the government employee done!

So, getting good insight from powerful people makes their life change and their entire generations

[3] 10 % of people

They are upper-middle-class people, they have everything in their hand

The common thing about these people are

▶ have a good amount of money

▶ luxury life

▶ always spent mode

▶ good circle but they misuse

▶ Bad habits

It's like I have everything but I misuse it because of my dopamine!

They can do some good jobs but they also create some disasters

But they enjoy their life as no known ever imagine.

When they have a mindset to help others, they will create a value

If they change their bad habits also lead a wonderful life

In simple words – this 10% of people JUST TRY.

[4] 9 % of people

They have everything they want, they are on the edge of the 1% people categories, and often they are millionaires

they have

▶ GOOD WORK ETHIC

▶ GOOD HABITS

▶ GOOD PEOPLES

▶ GOOD CIRCUMSTANCES

So, they didn't go the 1%

Because of sacrifices,1 % of people sacrifice heavier than you imagine, so it was hard for them to go long

Because they have committed schedules when they break everything is collapsed.

So, they need calculated risk tactics but often calculated risks fail because of their committed

When they need to develop into a new stage, THEY NEED TO SACRIFICE their comfort zone and good relationships .....

This is the reason, why 99% of people fail to reach 1%

IMPORTANT POINTS

I didn't recommend the 1% club route because it was not a path for red carpet road, it was the most dangerous path you ever imagine, and you have a lot of stress in your life

You didn't have a good relationship to spend your time, and if you have it was difficult to maintain it, which makes your family collapse

Just imagine the situation, where your daughter or son waiting for you at dinner but you have a business to run!!!!!

This was the condition that makes 9% into a separate column. So, only 1% of people who didn't have external family, but have an internal team in their life that leads them to create value in their life

Even 1% of people have families but again hard to manage !!!!!

These are the things that make man into separate levels

I didn't recommend anyone to anyone, because it was their life, their decision

1% want to create value in their life and others want to enjoy and also create some special thing in their life

You can live which life that you like, but your life creates value in the people's lives, once they feel the value created, YOU ARE SUCCEED

Conclusion

Nothing change, until you change,

Yeah! We are in the final part of the book, mm! I believe while you read this page, I think, you evolve from who you are from the beginning.....

The path of our lives depends on our circle of influences, so choose it carefully,

Little change in circumstances, not only affects you but also your generations

NEVER FORGET IT!

God doesn't create our destiny to be poor or hard, we just feel it but once you know the data and the core beliefs

I bet again again again again you !!!

you start to

THINK DIFFER

My prime motto is

TO INSPIRE OTHERS TO MAKE THEIR DREAM HAPPEN

I know I give you a spark,

then, CHOICE IS YOURS!!

But please, take it wisely

WE ARE LIVES ONLY ONCE IN THE WORLD!!!!

And one more, Emotions are part of our life, even failures or betrayals everything comes but don't influence this stuff to break your productivity

DO WHAT YOU LOVE TO DO

ALWAYS POSES HAPPINESS IN YOURSELF !!!

LIFE IS SHORT

ENJOY THE MOMENT

GO AHEAD AND DO SOMETHING BIG.

OK! MM!
See you guys
End with my favorite word – EVOLVE!

FOLLOW CG AT

TWITTER
INSTAGRAM
For any quires, WhatsApp at 8870098258
Mail at - entrepreneurcg11@gmail.com

Acknowlegement

I would like to thank my mentors, those who are the people, who open my eyes to a new lens of thinking that helps me to find my calling and my purpose of birth.

And my special thanks to my team members, whenever I feel depressed or stressed, these are the guys who step me upwards and boost my confidence

Another special thanks to Vishnu, irsath, sandy,nijju, and anath, who are my friends who act as my backbone of me, to help me to get a stable mood in my life.

My sincere thanks to my teachers in my college & school and my colleagues.

Thank you all of them to get a part of my life to design my destiny fruitfully!!!